BORN LEADER

THE STORY OF GUY GIBSON
DAMBUSTER

By

Alan Cooper

Published in 1993 by
Independent Books (London)
3, Leaves Green Crescent
Keston
Bromley BR2 6DN
Great Britain

First published 1993 by Independent Books (London)

A catalogue record for this book is available from the British Library

ISBN 1 872836 03 8

CONTENTS

PHOTOGRAPHS & ILLUSTRATIONS

Acknowledgements:

L W Collett, Ellen Warwick, Michael Gale, Janet de Gaynsford, Eve Gibson, Albert Postma, J Corrigan, Howard Jenkins, Keith Stretch, Air Cdr John Searby DSO DFC, Don Anderson, Bert Wrigglesworth, Selina Richardson, Jim Heveron MID, George Powell MID, Wg Cdr Danny Walker DFC*, Marna Young, Dave Rodger DFC, Sqn Ldr A C Neve MBE, Mrs F M Backhurst, Norman Mackenzie DFC, Hancocks & Co, Margaret Hull, Peggy Paterson, Roland Hammersley DFM, John Beynon, A J Condliffe, A P Purdy, Dorothy Mundon, Air Marshal Sir Harold Martin KCB DSO DFC AFC, Mrs Joan L Stiles, Mrs G Beeken, Joan E Civil, Mrs L G C Smith, Sydney, James Hawke, Ruth Gibson, St Edward's School - Oxford, Jim Verran DSO DFC, Mr Rudd, John Wilson, Gp Capt Rupert Oakley DSO DFC AFC DFM, Gp Capt R G Churcher DSO DFC* MVO, Gp Capt H Mahaddie DSO DFC AFC, Jim Marshallsay, A Denholm, Des Richards - 106 Squadron Association, R L Barnard, M R Sergeant, Molly Butcher, A Richards, W B Oliver DFC, Wg Cdr Tony Spooner DSO DFC, R G Low, Bert Combs, Sqn Ldr F E Harper, John Bryden MID, Richard James DFM, Brian Harris DFC, Wg Cdr Thompson DFC, Len Sumpter DFC DFM, W Howarth DFM, Jonathan Dimbleby, Kevin Whittacker, Macclesfield Historical Aviation Society, Derek Holloway, Dr Albath, Karl Schutte, Bob Gardiner, Rick Brand, 617 Squadron RAF, Public Records Office, Air Historical Branch, Air Crew Association, The Editor of Flypast, Imperial War Museum - Department of Photographs, Jackie Digges for her great help with typing and Hilda, my wife, for her patience and help whenever it was called for.

Sources:

Enemy Coast Ahead - Guy Gibson VC DSO DFC
Barnes Wallis - Morpugo
Als die Sperrmauer Brach - Roland Goock
Die Sinflut im Ruhtl - Joachim W. Ziegler

Abbreviations:

AC   - Aircraftman
Ai   - Air Interception (Airborne Radar)
AOC   - Air Officer Commanding
AP   - Aiming Point
BA   - Blind Approach
C in C   - Commander in Chief
Cpl   - Corporal
EA   - Enemy Aircraft
G.C.I.   - Ground Controlled Interception
H.E   - High Explosive
HQ   - Headquarters
IFF   - Identification Friend (or) Foe
KG   - *Kampfgeschwader* - Bomber Wing - *Luftwaffe*
LAC   - Leading Aircraftman
MT   - Motor Transport
OTU   - Operational Training Unit
P/O   - Pilot Officer
PRU   - Photographic Reconnaissance Unit
Sgt   - Sergeant
S/L   - Squadron Leader
VHF   - Very High Frequency
Wg Cdr - Wing Commander

1 - *Wing Commander Guy Gibson VC, DSO & Bar, DFC & Bar. Probably taken at Scampton after the Dams Raid (Imperial War Museum).*

CHAPTER ONE

THE EARLY DAYS

On 12th August 1918, in Simla, India, a boy was born Guy Penrose Gibson, Penrose being a Cornish name. In the history of World War Two the name, Guy Gibson, was to become, and still is today, a legend.

His father, Alexander James Gibson, who was the Chief Conservator of Forests for the Punjab, had been born in Russia in 1874. Alexander's father, James, had been born in Edinburgh, Scotland. Guy's mother, Leonora Mary (nee Strike), was born in 1894 at Porthleven, Cornwall. She came from a sea-faring family; her father, Edward Carter Strike, was a well-known Master Mariner and her mother, Emily Jane, (nee Symmons) was the daughter of a Master Mariner. They had five daughters and two sons, one of whom, Thomas Strike, followed in his father's footsteps. Guy's Uncle Thomas was a Master Mariner and served in World War I, being awarded the Distinguished Service Cross after taking on a German U-Boat in combat.

It was Edward and Emily, his grandparents, with whom the young Gibson was to spend a lot of his holiday time later on.

Alexander Gibson and Leanora Mary Strike were married on 2nd December 1913, at Fore Street Wesleyan Chapel, in Porthleven. It was said at the time to have been the most spectacular wedding ever to have taken place in the area. Soon after the wedding the couple left for India. In July 1915, their first child, Alexander Edward Charles, was born in Simla. Although named Alexander after his father he preferred, and became known as, Alick to all who knew him. In later life Alick was to find it difficult when his passport needed changing, having been born in India and having a father born in Russia. Their next child, a girl, Joan, was born on 10th August, 1917. Guy followed in 1918.

2 - Leonora and Alexander Gibson at their wedding.

Although there were three children from the marriage it was not a happy one, and certainly in Guy's later life the considerable age gap between Leonora and Alexander began to present more and more problems. These were apparently compounded by a drink problem Leonora developed, said to have been brought on by Alexander's roving eye for other ladies which was at the root of her unhappiness.

3 - Taken in India: Left to right Guy, Joan and Alick.

In 1924, the Gibson family returned to the UK and settled for a while in Porthleven at a house called *'South View'*. During their time in Cornwall they stayed in a number of places, including the Queen's Hotel, Penzance. From Cornwall they moved to London and stayed in a hotel in Kensington, the cost of which, for a week's full board, was only two pounds. Guy was a great help to the elderly ladies who were resident at the hotel, but the three children would also play pranks on them; much to the disgust of their mother. Their favourite playing spot in those days was the Round Pond in Kensington Gardens, though the holiday times were spent back in Cornwall.

Guy, Joan recalls, was a mischievous boy who could get into more trouble than the others but, to be fair, she also remembers he was very lovable and the first to stick up for anyone who needed it. On one occasion, having been in trouble, he locked himself in the bathroom and threw the keys out of the window. He had a little toy teddy which, in his own way, he talked to. He would say he, *'loved it so hard.'*

His first school was the West Cornwall College *kindergarten* for children up to the age of 8 years, where his headmistress was a Miss Hanna. From there he went to St. George's Prep School, in Folkestone, Kent and by this time it would appear his parents had returned to India. His later school holidays were spent with his grandmother in Cornwall. She was marvellous to the children, but eventually it got too much for her so Joan went to stay in a vicarage at St. Ives and the two boys lodged with an uncle. From there on the family were never quite as close as before, although they did keep in touch by writing and infrequent meetings.

When Guy was in Cornwall he would spend much of his time fishing with the local fishermen, or swimming in the harbour at Porthleven. He said: 'I think they enjoyed having a kid around; they told me good sea yarns while mending their nets.' On occasions they would take him out with them in the boats and brought home anything from dogfish to a conger eel. They would tell him of the mountainous seas, and of the ocean where men and gear were swept overboard. Guy's eyes would open wide in amazement, but he secretly enjoyed the fear that was in him.

He did spend one Easter holiday in Derbyshire, with an uncle who reared chickens. Guy and a cousin, Keith, were set the task of keeping an eye out for molesting birds. Armed with air rifles and singing and shouting loudly they went about their task. Their shots, as well as deterring the birds, also peppered some napkins which were hanging to dry in a neighbour's garden. It was some time before it was realised why they were full of small holes.

In September 1932, he went up to St Edward's School, on the Woodstock Road outside Oxford, with its acres of playing fields, five tennis courts, and a swimming pool. His brother, Alick, being older had gone up in 1930. Another future airman, Douglas Bader, had been there some eight years before. A warden at the school described Guy as being one of the most thorough and determined boys he had ever known, both at school and afterwards. The warden remembered Guy's determination to fly and also that he was, at first, rejected for the RAF owing to his short legs.

In 1935 he tried to see the famous test pilot Mutt Summers (who in later times was to feature much in his life and the Dambuster raid) but his first attempts failed until someone in his family, who knew Summers, wrote an introductory letter. Summers agreed to see him and Guy told him he was very keen to become a test pilot. The advice given by Mutt was 'Go and join the RAF and get as much flying in as possible, then come back and see me and we may be able to use you.' It was then that Guy was rejected by the RAF because of his height.

In the Second World War 150 boys from St Edward's school served in the Royal Air Force, of which forty-eight were decorated for their service and acts of bravery, and eleven were mentioned in despatches. The awards included one Victoria Cross (Gibson) and one George Cross. In 1954 the Air Council expressed their appreciation of the school's association with the RAF by granting £1,000 from the RAF Prize Fund to endow a scholarship of £40 a year for the son of a serving RAF Officer to attend the school. The scholarship was named after Guy Gibson.

Despite his short legs giving him slightly less than average height he eventually managed to get into the Royal Air Force,

4 - St. Edward's School Oxford. Gibson is centre left.

and reported to the Civil Flying School at Yatesbury on 16th November, 1936. On 31st January 1937, he was awarded a short term commission with the rank of acting/pilot officer and posted to Number 24 (Training) Group. The length of the commission was 4 years and it was back dated to 16th November 1936, the date he had first enlisted.

At 24 Training Group he spent a week getting kitted out etc. then, on 6th February, he was posted to Number 6 FTS Flying Training School at Netheraven for flying training. It was here that he began a short but full career learning to fly in the English weather conditions. He had a natural resilience which saved him from adolescent troubles and accidents. He had frequently been in car accidents with other drivers, but suffered no injury to himself. On one occasion he was in a car travelling at 70 mph across Salisbury Plain when the car crashed, turning over and over in the road. Gibson was thrown out and hit the road bouncing a number of times, but got up quite unhurt; in fact he was the only one in the car not injured. He said, 'I bounce you know!'

At Netheravon he was on Number 5 flying course and on 27th May 1937, a proud moment, he was presented with his wings, or to give it, its official title *'Flying Badge'*. On 4th September 1937 he was posted to his first operational unit, 83 Squadron at Turnhouse, Midlothian; it was part of No 2 Group of the newly formed Bomber Command. Later, when 83 Squadron moved to Lincolnshire, they were to come under 5 Group.

The aircraft of the day then was a Hawker Hind Bomber with a top speed of 185 mph, a range of 200 miles, and bomb carrying capacity of 500 lbs in various configurations. Gibson later went on to fly Blenheims, and Hampdens. On 27th September 1937, he went on a short parachute course with 24 Training Group at Yatesbury where he had begun his RAF career. This lasted until 2nd October and then it was back to 83 Squadron.

One person who recalled the young Gibson in those early days was Howard Jenkins. He had joined the RAF in March 1937 and, after training as a fitter, was posted to 83 Squadron in July, 1938. They had just returned from a summer camp in Scotland, and his first job was 120-hour inspections on the Hawker Hinds. In September 1938, when they were re-equipped with Handley Page Hampden bombers, the riggers and fitters were sent to Handley Page at Radlett to acquaint themselves with the aircraft.

When the first Hampdens arrived at the squadron the groundcrews, as was the practice in those days, were detailed to a particular aircraft. In Howard's case it was L4059 flown by the then Pilot Officer Guy Gibson. In May 1939, at a practice camp at Dingwall which had a hill, called the Friaries, at one end of the runway, Gibson took off, *'hanging the aircraft on the props'* as he backed away to avoid the hill. It was the most hair-raising thing Howard had ever seen, particularly as it was performed in a Hampden. On another occasion Gibson touched down on the road at the side of the perimeter and in so doing removed most of the fabric from the flaps, which had in fact only just been re-covered. In those days, still prone to be a little rash, he did fly a *'little close to the wind'* at times.

Gibson's next course was not until 19th February 1939, a short navigation course at Hamble. On 16th June 1939, he was promoted to Flying Officer. On 11th July, he flew a *'Fly the Flag Flight'* over France. It was a so-called training flight, arranged with the French, who, in turn, could fly over the UK in a similar manner. The flight on the 11th consisted of 100 aircraft, made up of Whitleys and Wellingtons, as well as Hampdens. His crew for this flight was Howard, who sat behind Gibson, and whose role it was to keep an eye on the instruments as, much later, the flight engineers did. The wireless operator/ come-air gunner was Jack Wilson. The plan was to take off from Scampton, fly to Tangmere to refuel and then take off for France at 11.00 hrs. The route would take them to Paris, Lyons, Avignon, and back the same way, the Whitleys and Wellingtons making a longer flight. After take off they flew south but soon ran into fog. Gibson tried to carry on but eventually had to turn back because conditions were impossible.

A few days later they took off again, but once more they encountered mist. Flying on for a while they came out of it and found themselves flying alongside a church steeple, later thought to have been Salisbury Cathedral; after which they once again turned back. A few more days passed and they took off in better conditions and reached Tangmere safely. After refuelling they took off on a lovely sunny summer's day and reached the Eiffel Tower, circling it at the height of the spectators' platform. The French people were waving to them and the rear gunner had a grandstand view. But by now, and has often happens in hot sunny conditions, things began to get bumpy with the rising hot air. The turbulence made the trip for Howard and Jack very uncomfortable and they were both sick out of the side of the aircraft.

Gibson was saving every drop of petrol he could on this flight by keeping his left foot jammed under the mixture control so that, when he throttled back, the mixture control on the Hampden would not come out to richen the mixture. Once again they circled the Eiffel Tower and then made for Tangmere, but Gibson decided to go straight on to Scampton and not to make the refuelling stop. This, of course, worried Howard and Jack because of the petrol situation. When they landed at Scampton they had been away nine hours, something of a record for the Hampden and Gibson had used every drop of *'juice'*. The next day, when the aircraft was refuelled, it was found the tanks were completely dry. This was an early indicator not only of Gibson's skilful airmanship, but also of his predisposition to stretch himself, his crew and his aircraft to the limit.

Gibson had been due to leave the RAF in April 1939[1], his four

---

[1] - *The four year engagement was backdated to 1936 when he first applied. He would only have served three years had the war not intervened.*

year engagement being up, and he wanted to get on and pursue his test pilot ambitions. He had accrued an impressive number of hours on both single and multi-engine aircraft and his knowledge of aerodynamics, a vital factor, was excellent. Hitler and Mussolini, however, had other ideas and as war was looming on the horizon all serving pilots were ordered to remain in the services for the duration of the forthcoming war. As far as the service chiefs were concerned war was an unavoidable fact, rather than a possible option. At the time Guy took a dim view of Hitler and what he stood for, but he had no worries about the forthcoming war.

In August 1939, he was on a sailing holiday at Saundesfoot, near Tenby, Pembrokeshire; he had spent a similar holiday there the year before. He stayed in a cottage with Mr and Mrs George Frost. George was a musician and played the piano in a local dance band and when he came home from a dance Guy would ask him to play his favourite tune, *'Deep Purple'*. George described Guy as a happy, carefree person. At the time Guy's favourite drinking place was the *'Hear Castle'* public house run by Mrs Waldron and her daughter.

Gibson had taken a small cat called *'Windy'* on holiday with him. *'Windy'* used to fly with him as his mascot and Guy would take him down to the beach each day and, no doubt, take him out in his sailing dinghy. He was out sailing one day when a young boy, whose parents he knew, swam out to him with a telegram. The message was brief and to the point, *'Return To Unit Immediately.'*

Soon after receiving the telegram he was taken by car to Oxford where he boarded a train for Lincoln, the nearest station to Scampton and 83 Squadron. On 29th August, he wrote to Mrs Frost, gave her his address and said that things were a bit grim, but as soon as things settled down he would be back for *'Windy'*. The letter was signed G P Gibson, Flying Officer RAF. He later decided that with a war coming he'd leave the cat with Mrs Frost for the duration, although he knew the cat would probably have forgotten him by the time it was all over. It would appear that he never did see the cat again, or at least only on occasional visits. However, whenever *'Windy'* heard an aircraft he would run up the apple tree or the clothes line as if he was looking for Guy. He went on to live to a ripe old age.

For Guy Gibson the war had begun. Little did he know then what lay ahead of him.

CHAPTER TWO

WAR IS DECLARED

At the time war became an inevitability Gibson was in 'A' Flight of 83 Squadron, the flight commander being S/L (Squadron Leader) Oscar Bridgeman. On 3rd September 1939 came the now immortal words of Neville Chamberlain, declaring that the UK was at war with Germany. This, of course, was not unexpected by the men of the Royal Air Force who had been on stand-by and preparing for war for some time. The crews were told by Bridgeman to test their aircraft and be prepared to get airborne. Gibson flew L4070-C, which he described as lousy, swinging on take off and with a tendency to dip the left wing.

On the very day war was declared, a Blenheim of 139 Squadron flown by F/O (Flying Officer) Andrew McPherson took off to photograph the German Fleet which was on its way out of Wilhemshaven. This was the first of 392,137 flights made by Bomber Command in WWII. At this time the command had 35 Squadrons and 638 aircraft, of which only 398 were twin engine. It was McPherson's photographs that prompted the battle order for six aircraft from 83 Squadron, three from 'A' and three from 'B' flights, to take the offensive immediately. The order stated:

> *'The greatest care is to be taken not to injure the civilian population. There is no alternative target'.*

Crews were forbidden to bomb targets on land for fear of killing French civilians.

The aircraft, carrying 4 x 500 lb. bombs set for a delay of eleven and half seconds, were ordered to attack the German ship *Von Scheer*, in the Kiel Canal area. Guy's crew, on this occasion, was P/O (Pilot Officer) Jack Warner, Sgt. Houghton

5 - The cockpit of the Handley-Page Hampden.

and AC (Aircraftsman) Hewitt (later in 1940 all aircrew had the minimum rank of sergeant). The operation was not a success, owing to bad weather, poor visibility and rain. So the bombs were jettisoned and the aircraft returned, Gibson landed at 22.30 hrs. A disappointment for 83 Squadron, but the ship was successfully attacked and damaged the next day by Blenheims and Wellingtons of No 2 Group.

6 - Gibson at his brother's wedding. Arm in sling due to 'flak wound'.

On 5th September, Guy attended his brother Alick's wedding in Rugby Parish Church as best man. Alick's bride was Rita Harris, whom the chaps on 83 Squadron thought was related to *'Bomber'* Harris, then AOC of No 5 Group (later to become Commander in Chief of Bomber Command). Needless to say Gibson did little to change that train of thought. He turned up at the wedding with his left arm in a sling and in his book, *'Enemy Coast Ahead'*, he states he had been bitten by the station commander's dog. But at the wedding he told Rita and Alick that he had been hit by shrapnel on his flight on the 3rd.

When he arrived back at Scampton he found the aircraft had

been sent to Ringway, which was thought to be safer than Scampton from enemy attack, a war footing plan arranged before the war started. After while in Ringway, near Manchester, Gibson was told to fly his aircraft back to Scampton, which for some reason or other he did not seem too keen to do. When he took off he made what was known as a *'Split Arse'* take off by opening both engines, which lifted the tail off the ground, then releasing the brakes, which made the tail of the aircraft swing. Consequently when the aircraft took off it went into an extremely strange angle. At the time workmen who were on top of a hanger, painting, threw themselves flat as Gibson's Hampden flew over very low.

He did a very fast circuit and then landed again. He told Howard Jenkins that the port engine was losing power which, he said, was the reason for his bad take off. The squadron leader who had given the intruction to fly to Scampton came out and asked Jenkins to run up and check out the offending engine. This he did, also the starboard, but could find nothing wrong. With that the squadron leader got in, took off and proceeded to beat up the airfield then landed. He then told Gibson in no mean terms to fly the aircraft back to Scampton, which he promptly did.

On 22nd December 1939, Gibson flew L4059 to St Athan to have the IFF (Identification - Friend from Foe) transmitter fitted. It should have taken a day and half, but the 24th came and still the aircraft was not ready. By then it looked as though he and his crew of Howard Jenkins and Jack Wilson would be spending Christmas there, especially as when they were eventually ready to take off, Jack realised his parachute was defective. Apparently some MT drivers had been fooling about with it and had accidentally pulled the release and had then just pushed the billowing canopy back inside its cover. Jack noticed it was not right and told Gibson, who said, 'If you're willing to fly without it we'll go.' Jack agreed, but then, as they taxied down the perimeter track, the wing hit a petrol bowser which had been parked too near the track. Gibson told Jenkins to go and check out the wing to see if it was cracked. It wasn't, just a bit bent, so they took off and flew back to Scampton.

7 - Gibson in the cockpit of his Hampden.

While they were up in Manchester a man came into the billet in which Howard Jenkins was staying and said what they thought was 'Who's guarding Manchester?' What he had actually said was, 'Who's guarding <u>the</u> Manchester', a newly designed bomber. After the initial confusion they asked 'What Manchester?' and were led off to a hangar where, in a screened-off portion, was the prototype Manchester bomber. At that time it had the two Rolls-Royce Vulture engines and nobody knew it would be quickly redeveloped into the four-engine Lancaster or how significant that aircraft would be.

In the meantime the war went on, although it was the phoney war period and leaflets, not bombs were being dropped. A leaflet raid could take anything from six to twelve hours, but a lot about weather and navigation was learned in those early days from operations such as this, and Gibson and his crew flew their fair share.

On 1st December 1939, Gibson went to a party in Coventry to visit his brother Alick, an officer of the 6th Battalion of the Warwickshire Regiment. It was there that he first met Eve Moore, an actress, who was at the time appearing in a play in Coventry called *'Come Out To Play'*, and who was later to become his wife.

In January 1940, 83 Squadron were posted up to Lossiemouth, in Scotland for anti-submarine work and it was from there that he took part in his next operation. On 27th February, they dropped a new weapon, a magnetic mine, which weighed 1,700 lbs and which, from then on, was called *'Vegetable'* (mine-laying operations were usually referred to as *'gardening')*. His crew was P/O Jack Withers, Sgt Houghton, and AC McCormack, the target was a rogue U-Boat returning from an Atlantic patrol in the area of Norway. A submarine was located and attacked, but it made a successful crash-dive and escaped. Perhaps as well for Gibson that it did, as it turned out to be British. They saw a second submarine, but did not attack because they thought it was British. It turned out to be the errant U-Boat. Some you win, some you don't!

On 29th February, the operation was a similar one with the same aircraft and crew, but on this occasion no sightings. It was while he was in Lossiemouth with 83 Squadron that Jenkins saw Gibson let down his hair for the first time. It was in the Queen's Hotel in Elgin, the nearest town to Lossiemouth, where Howard was surprised to see Gibson clamber up onto the grand piano and conduct the singing.

Guy also played in the station rugby team. S/L Stephen remembers playing for RAF Waddington against RAF Scampton and Gibson being in the team. The bulk of station teams, as it is still today, principally consisted of other ranks. In fact in 1940 the bulk of aircrew in the RAF were sergeant pilots, corporal navigators and wireless operator/air gunner airmen. There were only 800 or so permanently commissioned officers, of which, of course, Gibson was one. After the game it was the usual form to have tea in the corporals' mess and then retire to Lincoln and the local pubs. The favourite one, 'The Saracen's Head' is, sadly, no longer a pub but a ladies boutique.

Howard Jenkins remembers Gibson as being affable and a friendly, bouncy person who mixed well with everyone.

The Hampden was, he remembers, described as the *'Flying Panhandle',* mainly because of its shape and not its handling capabilities. In fact it was thought to be a nice aircraft to fly. The days leading up to 1940 were not promising, a patrol of Wellingtons on a patrol to Wilhelmshaven were jumped by German fighters and 12 out of 24 despatched were shot down. On 19/20th March 1940, the largest bomber force yet sent was despatched to attack a seaplane base at Hornum on the island of Sylt with 30 Whitleys and 20 Hampdens taking part.

A great tragedy in Gibson's life occurred at this time with the death of his mother at the tender age of forty-six. She had apparently run away from a home where she was undergoing treatment for her drink problem, and booked into a hotel in Kensington. It was there that she fell on an electric fire and suffered severe burns from which she later died. His father, at the time, was working at India House in the Strand as Parliamentary Science Secretary.

Guy's next operation was on 11/12th April 1940, a mining operation in Kiel Harbour, known as the *Fredrich Middlefart, Little Belt Kattegartd.* He took the same crew and the operation was from 2305 hrs to 0630 hrs. On 14/15th April he flew a similar operation, but on this occasion to the Middlefart Bridge area, Gibson recorded as having dropped the only successful mines from just 100 feet. There was only one change in his crew, P/O Watson for Sgt. Houghton, and his aircraft on this occasion was not L4070 but L4055. The trip lasted from 1845 to 0200 hrs. when a landing was made at Manston because of bad weather.

The objectives behind these attacks were threefold: first was to sink an enemy ship and block the harbour; second was to damage a number of ships, making them turn back or become grounded and, thirdly, and bluntly, to kill as many Germans as possible. It seemed to work because on 14th April a report showed that four enemy troop ships had been sunk and many of the troops lost in the area where the *'veg'* had been dropped by 83 Squadron between 11th and 15th April. On 20/21st April, the target was Aalberg airfield (occupied Denmark) and on this occasion his bomb load consisted of 30 x 40 lbs and 1 x 250 lb bombs. He had to change aircraft at the last moment because it was raining at the time of take off and rain had got into the intercom system making it u/s. Changing to a spare aircraft, 4049-A, he discovered the compass was not set correctly and he found himself over Copenhagen, in Denmark. He returned to Lossiemouth and landed at 07.55 hrs, having taken off at 23.55 hrs. On 23/24th April it was back to mine dropping, this time in the fjord at Oslo. Having successfully accomplished this he landed at Marham on return.

The Battle of Norway was now virtually over, the army had evacuated and the navy had a fierce sea battle, but were giving as good as they got. On 30th April 1940, a signal was sent by the C in C Bomber Command to the AOC of No 5 Group:

> *'Please convey to the squadrons in your group my appreciation and thanks for the splendid horticultural work done during the past month. It is gratifying to know that the seed they have so skilfully and conscientiously planted is already providing the enemy with much food for thought.'*

At this time the Commander in Chief of Bomber Command

was Charles Portal and the Air Officer Commanding No 5 Group was *'Bomber'* Harris. Together they were later to form a dynamic duo as Chief of the Air Staff and Commander in Chief Bomber Command. On 10th May, the handcuffs came off as far as Bomber Command were concerned, the phoney war was over. Mr Winston Churchill, First Lord of the Admiralty and soon to be Prime Minister, chaired a meeting of the War Cabinet at the Admiralty. It was decided that if the German invasion of Holland and Belgium was successful the RAF should attack the oil refineries and marshalling yards in those countries. Early on 13th May, General Rommel's 7th Panzer Corps crossed the Meuse near Dinant, the Germans were in France and the go-ahead was given to Bomber Command to begin an offensive on areas occupied by the Germans. The French Government were informed and the BBC instructed to broadcast an announcement accordingly.

Targets were selected with a view to help stop the German advance and cut off sources of supply. On 15/16th May, targets in the Ruhr were attacked but at this time Gibson and 83 Squadron were still involved in laying mines; on the 14/15th they dropped their lethal cargo off Copenhagen. On 16th May Churchill visited France and gave permission for heavy bombers to be used against the Meuse Crossings. The first attack was carried out on the 17/18th by 53 aircraft, while 78 others attacked Hamburg and Bremen; one of the aircraft detailed for Hamburg was flown by Gibson.

The target was known as A8, in those days every target had a letter and number, and it was the oil refineries that were to be attacked. The Germans had launched balloons in the target area and both flak and searchlights were thick on the ground. In a dive Gibson's aircraft hit a balloon cable which damaged the rudders, the starboard wing, and the compass. Gibson managed to fly it home, steering by varying the revolutions on his two engines. 'It sounds good when you tell it,' he said, 'but it is really very easy. You just use the throttles instead of the rudder!' Owing to fog at Scampton he had to land at Abingdon.

On 18th May, the King sent a message to HQ Bomber Command:

> *'I was able to hear about the epic deeds of our Bomber Force in recent weeks with the arduous and unceasing duties of Coastal Command and with the heroic deeds of our fighter squadrons in the country, and in France they make an immortal story, a story that fills the whole Empire whose sons are now fighting in all three branches. With gratitude and admiration I congratulate the RAF with all my heart and wish them good luck and continued success. The matchless spirit that has shown so clearly, an ascendancy over the enemy makes the final victory of the allies doubly sure.'*

Signed: *Geo R 18.5.1940.*

On 22/23th May, Gibson attacked a railway bridge over the Schelde-Mass railway and destroyed it, landing at Mildenhall on return. Ending a good month, on 26/27th May he attacked a railway tunnel on a line near Aachen by bouncing the bombs into it from a very low altitude. Some three years later, on a certain dam, he would be doing a similar thing.

The attack on 30/31st May was unsuccessful. The oil tanks 10 miles NE of Brunsbüttel could not be identified and, as the rule was that if you could not identify your target you brought back the bombs, the aircraft returned fully laden. On the morning of the 31st, Gibson was recommended for the DFC. Although at the time he would not have known, the recommendation was signed by A T Harris, Air Vice Marshal at HQ No 5 Group. It mentioned the trip when he hit a balloon and also the attacks on the railway bridge and tunnel. At the time he had completed 11 operational trips and 66 hours operational flying hours. This was approved by the King and gazetted on 9th June 1940.

The month of May had been an eventful one to say the least; the Army had been evacuated from France; Belgium requested an armistice on the 27th; the Battle of France had begun and all but ended and the Battle of Britain was about to begin. What the role of Bomber Command was to be became clear as soon as it became obvious Britain too would be fighting for her life.

Their main aim was to try and deprive the Germans of supplies and stop the movement of troops. On 13/14th June, Gibson made attack in the Ghent area; his log book states he was flying L 4070 his usual aircraft, but the operations book states it was L4106. On 17/18th June, his target was an oil refinery at Hannover, known as target A3; and so it went in June. The Principle Directive for Bomber Command dated 20th June 1940, gave the primary targets as; aircraft industries, communications, and mining, with oil as a secondary target. On the 21/22nd and 23/24th, in compliance with the directive, Gibson attacked aircraft factories at Kassel and Wismar. Then Wismar again on the 27/28th, both were attacked at low level and under intense flak defences.

In June 1940, the first Victoria Crosses in World War II were awarded to the RAF, both posthumously, to F/O Garland and Sgt Grey of 12 Squadron, flying a Fairey Battle, for an attack on a bridge over the Albert Canal on 12th May, 1940. On 10th June, Italy came into the war in alliance with the Germans, and on the 11/12th came the first raid on Italy. Thirty-six Whitleys attacked factories in Turin, refuelling on route in the Channel Islands.

France requested an armistice and on 25th June all hostilities stopped. On 1/2nd July, Gibson dropped the first 2,000 lb bomb in an attack on the *Scharnhorst* in Kiel. However the bomb missed the target and exploded in the town. The next day Gibson, flying P4402, attacked an oil refinery at Nantes; the whole area of the refinery was reported to have been ablaze with lights. On 4th July, came the first Anti-Invasion Directive. It seemed logical that as Hitler now dominated most of Europe he would now try and seize the UK as well.

The Principle Directive of 4th July detailed primary targets as: enemy ports, shipping which might be involved in an invasion, mining and the aircraft industry. Secondary was once again oil. On the 13th, the Directive changed again: the primary target becoming aircraft industries and, secondary, the inevitable oil. A footnote said that the whole bomber force was to be prepared to be diverted at short notice to the attack to repel an invading force. Another Directive on 24th July gave the primary as the *Luftwaffe* and the aircraft industry, and the secondary became communications. On the 30th, power, armaments, and chemical works became the primary targets.

————————————————

CHAPTER THREE

BATTLE OF THE BARGES

In June 1940, Air Vice Marshall Harris wrote to General Haining at the War Office; the letter concerned the number of barges that were available on the continent. It was estimated that some 500,000 barges, mainly driven by diesel engines, could be pressed into service if required. He went on to say that just 1,000 of these could transport a quarter of a million troops and that the largest Rhine barge, whilst not suitable for troops, could be used to convey ammunition and supplies. Converted barges with concrete floors could carry tanks and guns.

On 16th July 1940, Hitler issued Directive No 16 *'Preparation for the Invasion of England'*. The crossings would be on a broad front from the area of Ramsgate to an area west of the Isle of Wight; but first the Royal Air Force had to be reduced to a point where they could no longer mount an effective resistance. Next, the sea lanes would have to be swept cleared of mines, then the Straits of Dover were to be cut off on both flanks by new, thickly-laid minefields. In his memorandum of 12th July, General Jodl had called the operation *'Löwe'* (Lion) because it was seen as a fight against the British Lion. On the 16th it was given the new code name *'Seelöwe'* (Sea Lion). Directive No 17 came on 1st August 1940: *Die Luftwaffe* was to overcome the RAF with all means and in the shortest possible time - *Die Luftschlact um England*. The attacks were to be directed primarily against the aircraft themselves, then ground and supply installations and organisations, plus the aircraft industry. This was to begin on, or soon after 5th August.

Gibson did not fly many operations in August, but training was being undertaken in low level attacks on canals in Lincolnshire. In a low level attack against the Dortmund-Emms Canal on 12/13th August 1940, F/Lt *'Babe'* Learoyd of 49

Squadron was awarded the Victoria Cross[1] for just such an action. On 4th August, the Bomber Command Directive gave the targets as 'Objectives in Italy'.

The month of August 1940 was to be a dramatic one, although more so for Fighter Command. On the 10th, *Adlertag* (Eagle Day or Day of the Eagle), the main attack on the RAF stood ready. Göring announced it would take four days to destroy the defence works south of London and four weeks to destroy the RAF. This onslaught had been ready to start since the beginning of August but, because the weather forecasters could not predict a clear three days to begin, it was delayed for two weeks. On the 13th a number of bombers and fighters did take off despite the bad weather and attempts to recall them failed. An unescorted group of bombers hit Eastchurch airfield and in other areas German fighter escorts took off to find no bombers to protect. It was a bad start to the much vaunted *Adlertag* but the next day saw a more organised and effective effort.

On the 19th, at a conference in Germany, a Directive was issued by *Reichsmarshall* Göring. One of the things he said endorsed the effort and determination against the Royal Air Force, particularly the bombing sorties:

> 'As long as the enemy fighter defences retain their present strength, attacks on aircraft factories must be carried out under cover of the weather conditions permitting surprise raids by solitary aircraft. We must succeed in seriously disrupting the material supplies of the enemy air force by the destruction of the relatively small number of aircraft engine and aluminium plants.'

---

[1] - *First Bomber Command VC in WW II.*

He continued:

> 'There can no longer be any restriction on the choice of targets. To myself I reserve only the right to order attacks on London and Liverpool. Our first aim is the destruction of the enemy fighters. If they no longer take to the air we shall attack them on the ground, or force them into battle by directing bomber attacks on a growing scale. Once the enemy air force has been annihilated our attacks will be directed as ordered against other vital targets.'

On 20th August 1940, Winston Churchill delivered a speech to the House of Commons, a speech which was, arguably, to become his most famous speech of World War II. Over the years it has been quoted out of context, in fact the speech was 10 pages long and complimented the RAF as a whole, and not just the fighter pilots. We all praise their efforts and sacrifice and rightly so, but it was the effort of the whole of the RAF that made the winning of the battle, and preventing the invasion of the UK, possible. The full contents of the paragraph in which he complimented the RAF effort was as follows:

> 'The gratitude of every home in our island, in our Empire, and indeed throughout the world, except in the abodes of the guilty, goes out to the British airmen who, undaunted by odds, unrewarded in their constant challenge and mortal danger, are turning the tide of the world war by their prowess and by their devotion. Never in the field of human conflict was so much owed by so many to so few. All our hearts go out to the fighter pilots, whose brilliant actions we see with our own eyes day after day; but we

must never forget that all the time, night after night, month after month, our bomber squadrons travel far into Germany, find their targets in the darkness by the highest navigational skills, aim their attacks, often under the heaviest fire, often with serious loss, with deliberate careful discrimination, and inflict shattering blows upon the whole of the technical and war-making structure of the Nazi power. On no part of the Royal Air Force does the weight of the war fall more heavily than on the daylight bombers who will play an invaluable part in the case of invasion and whose unflinching zeal it has been necessary in the meanwhile on numerous occasions to restrain. We are able to verify the results of bombing military targets in Germany, not only by reports which reach us through many sources, but also, of course, by photography. I have no hesitation in saying that this process of bombing the military industries and communications of Germany and the air bases and storage depots from which we are attacked, which process will continue upon an ever-increasing scale until the end of the war, and may in another year attain dimensions hitherto undreamed of, affords one at least of the most certain, if not the shortest of roads to victory. Even if the Nazi legions stood triumphant on the Black Sea, or indeed upon the Caspian, even if Hitler was at the gates of India, it would profit him nothing if at the same time the entire economic and scientific apparatus of German war power lay shattered and pulverised at home.'

On 24th August 1940, came a dramatic moment in the war and probably changed the course of the *Battle of Britain* and, one could say, lost Hitler and Germany the war. On this day 550 German aircraft of *KG*2,3,4,26, and 27 attacked London for the first time since 1918. In daylight a total of 330 bombers attacked Dover, the south east coast and then swept in to the east end of London. The first wave of 75 aircraft attacked between 08.00 and 09.00 hrs and penetrated as far as Gillingham in Kent. The second wave of 85 aircraft attacked at about 12.30, raiding Manston airfield. The third wave of 70 aircraft attacked at 15.00 hrs in the east and west, as another 100 were attacking the Portsmouth and Southsea area.

The attacks on London were made in the area of Millwall docks where warehouses were damaged by fire. Any attacks on London had been forbidden by both Hitler and Göring but areas in Tottenham, Islington, Enfield, Hampton, Kingston, and up as far as Watford, were hit and damaged. In the City itself the West India Docks had No 11 warehouse damaged and Nos 3 & 4 were ablaze; the bombing seemed to be indiscriminate with no real targets in mind. It appeared that their designated targets were the petroleum depots at Thameshaven and the aircraft works at Rochester, but that the German bombers' radio direction finding apparatus (*Knickebein* - bent leg) was confused by the British radar counter-beams. It was later said that the crews who attacked London were, on the order of Hitler, transferred from the *Luftwaffe* to the infantry. In all 170 bombers are said to have attacked London on the 24th so it would appear that the ranks of the infantry swelled considerably after this date.

Earlier, in July, Churchill had laid down a plan to attack Berlin if ever London was bombed and as he watched the bombing of London from the top of the Imperial Chemical Building he must have been running the details through his mind. On 25/26th August, 103 Hampden and Whitley bombers set out to attack the *'Big City'*, as Berlin was later known to the aircrew. It was not so much the damage that these aircraft could inflict, but more the damage it would do to the morale of the German people that mattered; Göring had promised Hitler in 1939 that *'No enemy bomber would penetrate the Reich.'* It was the beginning of nine raids on the German capital between 25th August and the end of September. The target on the 25th was the Siemens and Halske factories and Siemens-Schubert factory, the power station at Klungenberg and the Templehof airfield. Number 5 Group, including Gibson's and other aircraft from 83 Squadron, despatched 41 Hampdens of which three failed to return including two that ditched in the sea; the other one crashed in East Anglia. Gibson himself refuelled as soon as possible to make a search for a ditched aircraft of 83 Squadron, only to find that after a long search they had in fact been picked up some while before. These were the only losses of the total force sent on the 25th and it is an indication of the element of surprise the attack inflicted on the Germans. The trips to the Berlin in the future months and years would not be so easy.

At the same time the Germans were making a return visit to London, this time bombing Bethnal Green. Also targeted were Birmingham and Newcastle plus an RAF Station in Yorkshire, which was attacked once again on the 26/27th. In return, between 24th June and 27th August 1940, 2806 tons of bombs were dropped by Bomber Command on a wide range of targets, the greater part on enemy airfields.

On 30th August, a photograph showed 52 barges in the Dortmund/Emms canal and that the length of each barge was 200 to 250 feet. It also showed the traffic on the canal was about three times heavier than on 1st August. On 31st August, Göring issued a staff instruction to his two air fleets to make frequent night reprisal raids on London. This was conceived as a blow against the political and economic centres of the British Empire, and at the morale of London's civilian population. So it was in fact the Germans who invented the *'Terror'* raids as they later called the RAF raids on their cities and towns. On 2nd

8 - Barges being assembled in preparation for Seelöwe.

September, Hitler issued a new order to the *Luftwaffe*, stating that attacks on the population and defences of the large cities, particularly London, were to be sustained both by day and by night. These were said to have been the first *Vergeltungsmassnahme* (reprisal measures) but were really an admittance of failure by the *Luftwaffe* High Command. On 3rd September, the anniversary of the outbreak of war, Churchill submitted a memo to the War Cabinet on the munitions situation:

> 'The Navy can lose the war, but only the Air
> Force can win it. Therefore our supreme effort
> must be to gain overwhelming mastery in the air.
> The fighters are our salvation, but the bombers
> alone provide the means of victory. We must
> therefore develop the power to carry on an ever

increasing volume of explosives to Germany, so as to pulverise the entire industry and scientific structure on which the war effort and economic life of the enemy depends, while holding him at arm's length in our island. In no other way at present can we hope to overcome the immense military power of Germany, and to nullify the further German victories which may be apprehended as the weight of their force is brought to bear upon African or Oriental theatres. The Air Force and its action on the largest scale must therefore, subject to what is said later, claim the first place over the Navy or the Army.'

He also suggested to the C-in-C Bomber Command that the bomber offensive should be spread as widely as possible over the cities and small towns in Germany.

On 4th September, Hitler made a speech ordering attacks on London to commence on 7th September. He said, 'If they attack our cities, then we will raze theirs to the ground. We will stop the handiwork of those air pirates, so help us God.' On this day 300 German bombers attacked London. Twenty-two large scale day and night attacks followed in the month of September. On the 6th September attacks on the ever growing force of barges assembled at the French Channel ports began, at Ostend, Flushing, Dunkirk and Calais. The attacks were at first made on the 7th by Blenheims and then by 26 Hampdens and eleven Fairey Battles whose targets were barges at Ostend and Calais. From then on through September 65% of the bomber effort was on anti-invasion targets, with 1,000 tons of bombs dropped. On 31st August, 18 boats had been observed at Ostend, by 7th September this had risen to 205.

On 8th September, Göring gave the code name Operation *'Loge'* (Lodge) to the attacks on London, and 625 bombers and 648 fighters attacked the City. Also on the 8th came the Invasion Alert No 1, code name *Cromwell*. On this day Gibson took off in Hampden X 2097 for an attack on the barges at Ostend. On the 13/14th September, the whole of the bomber force of 92 aircraft was directed against the barges. Observations and photographic evidence confirmed the barges were building up in number, and all could be used to transport troops and equipment.

Preparation was very much on the lines of the invasion by Julius Caesar in 55 BC.; he, of course, did not have to contend with being attacked from the air. Admiral Assman, a German historian, wrote of *'Seelöwe'* that the invasion on the south coast was to have begun on the 13th of August, but the bad weather precluded this until the end of the month. The British bombing and air attacks, together with the bad weather meant they had lagged behind schedule. The ten-day blocking of the Dortmund/Emms Canal caused by the bombing on 12th August, for which Learoyd was awarded the VC, held up the motorised boats coming from the Rhineland. In all, this meant *'Seelöwe'* being postponed from 15th September to the 21st, then the 24th, and then again to the 27th.

On 15th September, 155 aircraft were despatched to attack barges at Antwerp, the same night the Germans attacked London, Southampton, and Portland. Considerable damage was done to the shipping in Antwerp and elsewhere. Gibson was on the raid with 83 Squadron in his old faithful L4070 and attacked the barges from 800 feet and a direct hit was observed. It was during this trip that Sgt John Hannah, at the tender age of 18, for his courage was awarded the VC. He was flying with P/O Connor, a Canadian, in P 1355 when the aircraft was hit by anti-aircraft fire, and a fire started; both the petrol tanks were pierced and in danger of exploding. For a while Gibson flew alongside and could see in the light from the flames that it was a 83 Squadron Hampden. Hannah fought to put out the fire with everything he could put his hands on, including his flying log book whilst Connor struggled to control the badly damaged aircraft. The heat was so intense inside that the two carrier pigeons carried had been roasted alive, but Hannah refused to be beaten back, allowing Connor to get the aircraft back for a safe landing at Scampton.

It was Hannah's 11th operation with 83 Squadron and on the following day John, who came from Paisley in Scotland, was recommended for the VC; the recommendation was endorsed by Air Vice Marshal Harris on the 17th, and immediately approved by the King. He was decorated at Buckingham Palace on 10th October 1940, three days after leaving hospital. John Hannah saw the war through but, sadly, on 7th June 1947 he lost his last battle and succumbed to TB. John, who was then still only twenty-five left a widow, Janet, who later presented his VC to the Squadron at Scampton. Connor was awarded the DFC for his part in the valiant effort but was to die only a few months later after his aircraft had crashed into the sea. His body was found floating in a dinghy some way off shore. He is buried in Brattleby near Scampton.

On the 20th, Gibson flew on another operation to Antwerp and on this occasion an anti-aircraft shell entered the aircraft without exploding. It entered through the floor near the rudder bar, smashing it and knocking out Sgt Houghton, the bomb-aimer. Gibson kept the remnants of the rudder bar in the squadron office along with other bits and pieces he had collected. His experiences were certainly varied, on one occasion he chased a Dornier 17 bomber down a valley in Lorient, in France, and saw it disappear behind some trees. It was credited to him as a *'probable'* shot down.

From the beginning of the war to 12th September 1940, the Germans had dropped some 11,000 tons of bombs on the UK but despite this the Germans did not seem to know the importance of attacking specific targets. On 19th September, the C-in-C of the German Armed Forces, General Keitel, said air attacks on London would be carried out over a wider area, and from a military point of view. Terror raids would only be carried out as a last resort. On 22nd September, the AOC of No 11 Fighter, Group AVM Keith Park, admitted that if the attacks had not been switched to London from the fighter airfields they could not have survived.

In contrast, on 21st September, came a new Directive for Bomber Command Anti-Invasion Operations against major concentrations of barges in enemy ports, the secondary targets being the German Air Force, industries and oil. The aims of the British Bomber Command were clearly more specific and, as it was later to become apparent, much more effective because of it.

By the 21st September 1940, the attacks by Bomber Command had resulted in the destruction of 12 transport ships, 4 tugs, 51 barges, and 9 transports. Listed as damaged were 1 tug and 163 barges. On 23rd September, Gibson went to Berlin to attack the Potsdam Power Station. Churchill felt that power stations were important targets and could, if knocked out, cripple a city. It was to be Gibson's last operation with 83 Squadron and his last bombing operation for some time. 129 aircraft took part, S/L Oscar Bridgeman, a flight commander with 83 Squadron, went missing, but later turned up as a prisoner of war.

The Battle of the Barges was over and the invasion was postponed indefinitely by Hitler. Failure to nullify the RAF's defences and the fact that the transport for the invasion was being destroyed had foiled Hitler's plans to invade the UK. When the Battle of Britain is talked about in the years to come, so also must the Battle of the Barges be spoken of in the same context as they go hand in hand.

CHAPTER FOUR

FIGHTER PILOT

With the battle of the barges over and the threat of invasion receding Gibson took stock of his situation. He had heard there was a shortage of night fighter pilots and volunteered for training. On 26th September 1940, he was posted to No 14 Operational Training Unit at Cottesmore, then, on 11th October, to No 16 OTU at Upper Heyford. On 13th November, he was posted to 29 Squadron based at Wellingore in Lincolnshire, a satellite of Digby, which the aircrew called 'WC1'.

At the time 29 Squadron were operating with Blenheims as night fighters but were soon to convert to the Beaufighter, which was much more suited to the role. Gibson made his first flight in a Blenheim L1303 on 15th November, and his first sortie, known as an 'X' Raid Patrol, on the 19th. In his flying log book he was certified as a first pilot for the purposes of day flying on the 16th, and for nights on the 19th, the day of his first sortie. On this operation he had as his crewman P/O Watson.

At 29 Squadron he was made 'A' Flight Commander, not a popular choice as far as the 29 Squadron men were concerned, particularly as he had formerly been a *'Bomber Type'*. Apparently the man they had hoped to get was F/O Charles Winn (who later went on to be Air Vice Marshal Winn CBE DSO DFC). Winn was the senior pilot on the squadron and very popular and when they heard Gibson was coming, with no background on fighters, they were dumbfounded. P/O Don Anderson, a pilot with 29 Squadron, was in the ante-room at 'The Grange', a rambling old house in the village used as the officers' mess, when Gibson arrived. The reception he got was cool to say the least, owing to the controversy over his appointment over Winn. The atmosphere was broken by two other newcomers to the squadron: P/Os Graham-Little (later killed with a Mosquito squadron) and Davidson. Gibson, in his book, mentions they were the first to speak to him. They took him to the bar for a drink, but the rest ignored him. However Gibson's character and his skill as a pilot soon won over the other pilots and all was well. Winn, to his great credit, helped this by flying under Gibson's command in 'A' Flight.

Mr Barnard[1], a corporal engine fitter with 29 Squadron at the time, clashed with Gibson over the treatment the engines of his aircraft. It had just undergone a 90 hour check and Corporal Barnard was responsible for running up the engines before returning to the flight. One of the checks was to drain the carburettors on the Hercules engines and check for dirt or other foreign bodies. Gibson was standing by on the tarmac at the time and seemed to object to the engine being 'banged' (backfiring due to a weak mixture) whilst starting due to temporary fuel starvation. Apparently he climbed on the aircraft and asked Barnard what the hell he was doing to his aircraft! That aside, ex-Corporal Barnard remembers Gibson as a dedicated and first rate airman. He also remembered, later, Eve performing in the 'Merry Wives of Windsor' for the personnel after the squadron had transferred to West Malling.

On 21st November, Gibson, with P/O Lovell as his passenger, flew down to Cardiff in Blenheim L1502 to be married to Eve - Evelyn Mary Moore. The marriage to took place on the 23rd at All Saints Church, Penarth, a seaside resort west of Cardiff. His father, Alexander, was present as was Eve's father, Ernest Edward Moore. Eve was small and fair and had the trim figure of a dancer, which, as well as being an actress, she was. Guy is said to have liked her because she could talk. 'It was nice,' he once said, 'to meet a woman who could talk to you about books and music.' She was six years older than Guy but that didn't seem to matter. After a honeymoon in Penarth he got permission

[1] - *See photograph on page 54*

to live out, and he and Eve lived in the local village pub, the 'Lion and Royal'.

9 - Eve and Guy at their wedding.

10 - The wedding group.

11 - Guy and Eve on their honeymoon at Penarth.

Gibson first flew a Beaufighter (R2144) for 45 minutes on 1st December 1940 to get the feel of the aircraft. His first operational flight was on the 10th with Sgt Taylor in R2150 and this time he logged one hour and five minutes. They reported chasing a blip on their radar screen for 20 minutes, but because of icing he had to give up the chase. The blip was later identified as friendly. On the 11th, at 07.50 hrs Gibson, again in R2150, was ordered up on an 'X' raid. He chased a bandit out over the sea and eventually fired at it with two short bursts from about 800 yards range in a position about 60 miles east of Maplethorpe. Gibson identified the target as a Junkers Ju88, reporting that it did not return fire and no strikes were discernable on the EA (enemy aircraft).

On 15th December he was certified as a first pilot for day and night flying on the Beaufighter, a formidable machine at the time with its four 20mm cannons and six machine guns. On the 20th, he reported seeing a Heinkel He 111, and on 8th January 1941, he flew P/O Don Anderson on type experience on the Beaufighter. The flight, according to Gibson's log book, lasted 20 minutes.

Gibson, appeared to some to be bumptious and somewhat cocky, but Don Anderson remembered a good relationship with him. They were all trying to do their best within the limitations of aircraft and equipment and Gibson, he felt, was not immune to those frustrations. Don also recalled that Gibson liked a party or booze-up, but then most aircrew at the time did; it didn't make him a drunkard and it certainly did not affect his flying. On 2nd February 1941, S/L Widows was promoted to wing commander and it was expected he would be posted because fighter squadrons were commanded by squadron leaders (whereas a bomber squadron was commanded by a wing commander).

On 4th February 1941, flying with Sgt RH James, his Ai (airborne radar) operator, Gibson attacked an enemy aircraft between Grimsby and Spurn Head. They were not certain of its

FIGHTER PILOT

INTELLIGENCE COMBAT REPORT.

Sector Serial No. .... (A) W.C.1

Serial No. of Order detailing Flight or Squadron to
Patrol .... (B) 50

Date .... (C) 4/2/41

Flight, Squadron .... (D) Flight : "A" Sqdn. : 29

Number of Enemy Aircraft .... (E) ...... One or Two.

Type of Enemy Aircraft .... (F) ...... Uncertain.

Time Attack was delivered .... (G) 1955 - 2005 hours.

Place Attack was delivered .... (H) Between Grimsby and Spurn Head.

Height of Enemy .... (J) 7,000 to 10,000 feet.

Enemy Casualties .... (K) ...... NIL.

Our Casualties .... Aircraft ...... (L) ...... NIL.

Personnel .... (M) ...... NIL.

GENERAL REPORT. Searchlights. (R) (X.1) NIL.

.... (X.2) NIL.

Aircraft Fire- Range & length of bursts. (S) 1st attack 3 seconds at
500 yards range. 2nd attack
3 seconds from 800 yards.

General Report (R) One Beaufighter took off
from W.C.1 at 1839 hours to patrol base at 10,000 feet. At 1900 hours
Beaufighter was vectored to Mablethorpe area and at 1202 got a blip
on A/I while investigating a flair. At 1919 an a/c was seen in
searchlights ahead but on investigation proved to be another
Beaufighter. Search was continued in the area between Grimsby and
Spurn Head where flares were seen to be dropping. By coming up
behind and below a line of about six flares the enemy aircraft was
seen above and ahead illuminated dimly by the flares below it at
about 1955 hours. Fire was opened at 500 yards range giving a 3
second burst. E/A was lost to sight when flares went out but had been
picked up on A/I meanwhile and was held and followed for a few seconds.
No apparent avoiding action was taken by enemy which was lost in
turns. The flares appeared to ignite about 1,000 feet below the
aircraft and burned for about 15 seconds, being dropped in rows of
six and very bright. The aircraft type could not be determined as
it appeared as a dull silhouette and distinguishing features could
not be seen.

Signature   (Continued overleaf).

O.C.   { Section
             Flight
             Squadron   Squadron No.

when visual contact was established with an a/c about 400 yds ahead of the Beaufighter. The pilot identified this a/c as a HE 111, and closed to about 100 yds range and fired a short burst from dead astern. The pilot considers it probable that this burst killed the rear gunner since no return fire was received from the H.E.111. The guns of the Beaufighter then jammed but the H.E.111 was followed until the stoppages were cleared when a second short burst was given from about 50-100 yds range from dead astern, this fire stopped the Port engine of the H.E.111. Two further short bursts of fire from the same range and position stopped the Starboard engine of the H.E.111 and a large fragment from the engine struck the wing of the Beaufighter and dented it. The H.E.111 was at this time losing height at the rate of 1,000 ft. per minute. The Beaufighter followed the H.E.111 down and saw it go into the sea in a position about 2 miles off Skegness at 22.09 hours. Previously the pilot had seen one member of the crew bale out - The searchlights confirm that an a/c (either a H.E.111 or Ju.88.) crashed into the sea in the above position and at the same time.

The Beaufighter landed at W.C.1. at 22.21 hours. The weather at the time was clear with bright moonlight and no low cloud.

Reflector sight used Type G.J.3.
No cine-gun carried.
Number of Rounds fired - Starboard outer   7
                         "   inner   60
              Port   outer   3
               "   inner   756

               Total   126

Cause of stoppages not yet determined.

Pilot. F/Lt. G.P. Gibson, D.F.C.

A.1. Operator Sgt. R.H. James.

H. C. J. Browning
            F/O

Intelligence Officer, 29 Squadron.

type but Gibson fired 63 rounds with no damage observed on the enemy. On 14th March, once again with Sgt James and while patrolling at Wells, he picked up a blip in the area of Skegness, which he held for about 10 minutes. Visual contact was made at about 400 yards and positively identified as a He III. Firing the first burst at about 100 yards he thought he had killed the rear gunner because there was no return fire from the Heinkel. He then had a stoppage in his guns but continued to follow the enemy until it had been cleared. The second burst hit and stopped the EA's port engine, two further bursts hit and stopped the starboard engine and a piece of wreckage come off, hitting and denting the Beaufighter's wing. They followed the He III down as it lost height at the rate of 1000 feet per minute, until it was seen to hit the sea about 2 miles off Skegness Pier at 22.09 hrs. Only one member of the crew was seen to bale out. In all Gibson fired 126 rounds in the combat. The next day he went over to the area and was given the Heinkel's dinghy which he later used on visits to Cornwall.

On 8th April, the roles were reversed and it was he who was on the receiving end of an attack. On returning from an 'X' Raid and about to land on 'finals', an enemy aircraft, later identified as a Ju88, dropped in behind them from slightly above and opened fire. A cannon shell went through the Ai set and wounded Sgt Bell, who was on loan from 219 Squadron, in the leg. Other shells exploded in the aircraft damaging the hydraulic system. With its brakes useless it ran off the end of the runway, through a hedge into a field beyond.

On 23rd April, Gibson was back with Sgt James again and picked up blips east of Boston which turned out to be a Dornier 17. The engagement had to be broken off for a while owing to the accuracy of the return fire from the enemy's rear gunner. Closing to about 150 yards Gibson opened fire with two short bursts and hits were observed on the fuselage, but because of more accurate fire from the Dornier he broke away and it was lost. When Gibson landed at 01.30 hrs a dent was found on the

BORN LEADER

COMBAT   REPORT.

Sector Serial No. ....(A) WC2

Serial No. of Order detailing Flight or Squadron to
 Patrol...(B) ... WO - 1 O

Date ....(C) 14/3/41

Flight, Squadron ....(D) Flight: A .... Sqdn.: 29 ....

Number of Enemy Aircraft................................(E) .... One

Type of Enemy Aircraft...(F) .... H. 111

Time Attack was delivered............................(G) Final attack about 2203 hours

Place Attack was delivered............................(H) Final attack about 3 miles off
                                                                                 Skegness

Height of Enemy...(J) ...13,000

Enemy Casualties ....(K) ...Destroyed One HE. 111

Our Casualties ....Aircraft.........(L) .... Nil

                        Personnel..............(M) .... Nil

GENERAL REPORT *Searchlights* ....(N.1) N/A

A.A. Guns ....(N.2) N/A

Aircraft Fire :- Range & Length of Bursts (P)o-100 yds range - 4 burst each
General Repat. .... (R) about 2 secs duration.

One Beaufighter of 29 Squadron left W.O.1 at 1946 hours to patrol Skegness at 1200 ft.
The Beaufighter was handed over to Orby control, and carried out patrol over Wells
area from about 2026 hours till about 2027 hours when the Beaufighter was directed
after a raid to the east in vicinity of Skegness. Subsequently the Beaufighter
was directed after a raid in vicinity of Bircham Newton and this raid was followed from
about 2049 hours for about 15 minutes in westerly direction. No visual contact
was made. The Beaufighter was thene directed in an Easterly direction towards
a raid proceeding in a Northerly direction over the Wash. At about 2130 hours a "Blip"
was obtained on the A.I. and was held for about 10 minutes then visual contact

.   Signature   Overleaf/

           O.C. { Section
                   Flight
                   Squadron   Squadron No.

Using similar tactics the same or a second aircraft was
picked up by sight at 2005 hours. A 3 second burst from 200
yards range was given and the E/A was again followed for a
short period on A/I.

No return fire was experienced and no damage to the E/A
was observed during either of these attacks which were carried
out between 7,000 and 10,000 feet.

Reflector sight used. Type G.J.3.

Equipment functioned satisfactorily.

```
No. of rounds fired : Port outer  - 40
              "       inner  -  1  Cocking lever left down.
           Starboard outer- 21  Slow rate of fire.
              "       inner  -  1  Cocking lever left down.
                             ----
                      Total   63
                             ----
```

Pilot of Beaufighter :   F/Lt. G.P. GIBSON.

A/I Operator :   Sgt. R.H. JAMES.

Weather very clear, no cloud, half moon.

Beaufighter landed at ".C.1 at 2115 hours.

E. A. Olty.

                                       F/Lt.
              Sector Intelligence Officer.

outboard of the starboard nacelles, thought to have been caused by a piece of the Do17. He was credited with it being damaged and had fired 200 rounds.

On 29th April, 29 Squadron moved to West Malling in Kent, flying down in a formation of eight aircraft. On 7th May, west of Shoreham, an enemy aircraft was picked up in an area of patrol that had been given to Gibson by the Biggin Hill Controller, code-name *Anteater*. Having homed in on the blip he came to visual range and raised the aircraft's nose, firing a two second burst. Almost immediately the EA began breaking up and bits began falling everywhere. Gibson then saw exhaust flames and was about to open fire again when the enemy aircraft erupted in flames and crashed near a house north of Bognor.

12 - 29 Squadron at West Malling 1941. Corporal Barnard is sitting in the second row 4th from the right. Gibson was not present.

On 10th May, whilst flying on patrol over the Thames Estuary, Gibson came upon four He111s all bombed-up and heading for their targets. Richard James recalled that they had been ideally positioned and had clear visuals on the bombers.

FIGHTER PILOT

YEAR 1941		AIRCRAFT		PILOT, OR 1ST PILOT	2ND PILOT, PUPIL OR PASSENGER	DUTY (Including Results and Remarks)	SINGLE-ENGINE AIRCRAFT			MULTI-ENGINE AIRCRAFT					PASS-ENGER	INSTR./CLOUD FLYING
Month	Date	Type	No.				DAY Dual / Pilot	NIGHT Dual / Pilot		DAY Dual / 1st Pilot / 2nd Pilot		NIGHT Dual / 1st Pilot / 2nd Pilot			Dual / Pilot
May	1	BEAU	2250	Self	Sgt James	AI and Local. *Totals Brought Forward*				1·10					
	2	"	"	"	"	Sector Recco. A.L.				2·00	2·10				1·00
	3	"	"	"	"	N/F Test.				·10					
	5	"	"	"	Solo	X Raid Patrol. Nothing.				·15					
	5	"	"	"	F/Sgt Lamey	A/T Test.				·15					
	7	"	"	"	Sgt James	Test				·35					
	7	"	"	"	"	AI Practice									
						X Raid - One destroyed									
						By Lucky Burst. It blew up									
						Another Did the same before									
						I could open fire.									
	9	"	"	"	"	AI Practice.				1·00	3·05				1·30
	9	"	"	"	"	X Raid Patrol. Stooging.				·20	2·45				1·30
	10	"	"	"	"	N/F Test.									
	10	"	"	"	"	X Raid Patrol. A Blitz									
						On London. Saw Two									
						He III - but couldn't									
						Would not reg. damaged									
						One with Brownings - Follow									
	11	"	"	"	"	N/F Test. Cannons would not				·26	8·35				2·00
	13	"	"	"	"	N/F Test. } not				·25					
	13	"	"	"	"	N/F Test. } Fire				·15					
	15	"	"	"	"	Air firing again - No4.				·45					
						Cannons O.K.									
	19	"	"	"	"	All fired.				·55					

GRAND TOTAL (Cols. (1) to (10)) .... Hrs. .... Mins.   TOTALS CARRIED FORWARD

55

Gibson pressed the 'Fire' button for the cannons but nothing happened. Committed to the attack he switched to the Browning machine guns and managed to damage one of the enemy aircraft. Richard James plotted it going all the way down on his Ai but it was not confirmed as a 'kill'. The suspect cannons were tested over the next four or five days and worked without fail until the very last test when once more they failed to fire. The fault was then traced to a defective electrical solenoid. 'They were four very lucky bomber crews,' said Richard.

Richard James recounted another occasion which was not recorded in Gibson's log book when they did a little 'freelancing'. They had been overflying the Channel and were in the Dunkirk area when a huge searchlight was spotted being trained on the cliffs of Dover. Gibson asked James if he thought they should put it out and he agreed they should. Dropping height they flew in low and fast with all guns and cannon ablaze; the light soon dimmed and went out but up came a wall of flak. However the Beaufighter was so low that the shells burst well above them and they escaped unscathed.

It was whilst Gibson was with 29 Squadron at West Malling that he acquired is dog, Nigger, who was to figure strongly in later days and was to become his constant companion. A bitch belonging to one of the other pilots had had a litter and Gibson chose Nigger. A Maltese Cross type medallion was made up of duralamin and inscribed 'Nigger - 29 Squadron'. However this became detached from the dog's collar when the securing ring wore through the soft metal and was only found by one of the groundcrew after both dog and master had left the squadron. The finder gave the medallion to Richard James[1] who, in turn, passed it on the RAF Museum along with his own flying log book.

On 29th June 1941, Gibson was given the acting rank of squadron leader, and on 1st December was made temporary squadron leader. On 7th July, he shot down a He111 off Sheerness: after closing to 50 yards and opening fire, the German aircraft caught fire and was seen to crash in the sea. His log book at the end of July showed three enemy aircraft destroyed, one probable, and one damaged. On 12th July 1941, Sgt Richard James, Gibson's Ai operator, was recommended for the DFM, having flown 105 operational night flying hours with him. The recommendation mentioned the successful combats, and that he had proved to be an inspiration to the other Observers/Radio operators on 29 Squadron.

On 21st August, Gibson was recommended for a bar to his DFC, a full account of his combats and time with 29 Squadron were recorded in the recommendation. The award was approved by Air Vice Marshal Leigh-Mallory AOC No 11 Group, by Air Marshall Sholto Douglas C-in-C Fighter Command, and the King. The award was gazetted on 16th September, 1941.

On 21st October, Gibson saw and damaged two Ju87s off Dover. In his log book, on 28th December, it is recorded that as a night fighter pilot and in air gunnery he was above average. However his time as a fighter pilot was drawing to a close. On 23rd December, he was posted to No 51 OTU at Cranfield as an instructor, having flown 99 sorties as a fighter pilot. During the early months of 1942, he flew all manner of aircraft; Lysanders, Dominies, Oxfords, Wellingtons, and so on, finally taking over the position of chief flying instructor. He stayed until he was posted to HQ No 5 Group awaiting a posting on 23rd March, 1942.

He had gone to fighter command for a rest and a change after his bombing operations, but now he was anxious to get back from whence he had come, and where he really felt he belonged. His wishes were soon to be fulfilled as he soon received a telegram asking him to report for an interview with the newly appointed C-in-C Bomber Command, 'Bomber' Harris. The interview must have gone well as two days later another telegram arrived telling him he was to command 106 Bomber Squadron at Coningsby, in Lincolnshire. On 13th of April 1942 he arrived at 106 Squadron for his first command.

13 - The end of a successful partnership. Gibson shakes hands with Richard James under the nose of 'Admiral Foobang III' (Richard James).

FIGHTER PILOT

1. *At the time of writing this book Richard James is in his eighties and is shortly to make a pilgrimage to Gibson's grave in Holland and took the time to reflect on the many 'Ops' he flew with him. He has said that many people seem to think Gibson was hell-bent on chasing 'Gongs' (medals), people who didn't know him. Richard dispelled that idea completely by saying quite categorically that he found Gibson to be a very careful and considerate pilot who did not take unnecessary risks. He was not one of those aircrew who just did their job and no more, but was one who looked beyond that to ways of winning the war. He was too dedicated to what he was doing at the time to talk about 'after the war'.*

CHAPTER FIVE

TO COMMAND

Guy Gibson arrived at Coningsby for his first command, having been a flight commander and having been awarded two DFCs, one with Bomber Command and one with Fighter Command. He had arrived back in Bomber Command at an interesting period; there was the new C-in-C, Air Chief Marshal Sir Arthur Harris, and at that time the actual role of Bomber Command seemed to be in doubt. The Navy was running Coastal Command and wanted as many aircraft as they could get, Harris was having to fighting to save what he had, let alone try to get more! By 1942 Bomber Command had few more aircraft than they had in 1939. As things were it looked as though would be some time, if ever, before an effective bomber force could be assembled to mount any form of offensive action.

When Gibson arrived at 106 Squadron they were operating with the infamous Manchester bomber, the prototype of which Howard Jenkins had seen 1940. At that time it was hoped that it would be the answer to Bomber Command's problems. However, being seriously underpowered by its two Rolls-Royce Vulture engines it was a disaster of an aircraft. It was generally felt that anyone who flew in it and survived was lucky.

Gibson took over 106 Squadron from Wing Commander Bob Allen DSO, DFC and Bar. His first flight in a Manchester was on 1st April in L7485 with F/Lt Robertson (later 'A' Flight Commander). Although his posting was not official until the 13th, he had gone over before hand to get a feel of things while Allen was still in command. His promotion to war substantive squadron leader and acting wing commander came on 13th April, the day he was officially posted in, and he made his first operational flight on 22nd April, a mine laying trip recorded in his log book as 'Gardening - Radishes'. The trip in L7418 was uneventful dropping six mines in Kiel Harbour. He found the

Manchester heavy after the Beaufighter and he appeared, since his sojourn into Fighter Command, to want to fly bombers with the agility of fighters, or at least he tried to.

On the 25th the target was Rostock, on 4th May it was 'Gardening - Rosemary' and on 8th May the Heinkel Works at Warnemunde. Gibson, flying in R5770, along with 192 other aircraft, bombed from 3,500 feet and got good results. At the same time the crews of 106 Squadron were recorded as having bombed the Heinkel works, the Germans were in the UK bombing Bath with 150 aircraft. The raid on Rostock brought an outcry from Hitler in which he threatened 'Eradication' of all British cities, one by one. This had been the third attack on Rostock in as many days and, as a result, a substantial flak presence had been drafted into the area, making the defences formidable. One wonders, as did the crews of 106 Squadron at the time, why the town was not demolished in the first attack when the defences were very light. Nonetheless the losses were comparatively light, only 8 aircraft missing out of a total of 521 aircraft despatched.

At this time points were awarded for aiming point pictures: the pictures taken directly after the bombs had been dropped. In 106 Squadron people such as 'Bunny' Grein, 'Wimpy' Wellington, 'Ginger' Crowfoot, etc were bringing back excellent aiming photographs and the squadron was number seven in the running order of points scored. The ever growing problem was to gain accuracy and to hit the designated targets. If one could knock them out in one go it would save a lot of time and effort, and above all else, lives. The three great problems still to be solved were:

(i) Could the defences of a vital industrial area be 'saturated' by a similar operation on a much larger scale;

(ii) Were the high concentrations, now seen to be

desirable, a practical proposition;

(iii) How could the weather limitations on finding
and marking the target be overcome?

The Pathfinders, formed on 11th August, were to cover the
last problem (iii). Their role was to go in ahead of the main
force and mark the target area with flares, or pyrotechnics as
they were known. The device known as 'Gee', or T.R. 1335 to
give it its official title, had been first used on 8th, 9th and 10th
March, 1942, the technique having been perfected by 115
Squadron and then by 1418 Flight. However it had a limited
range of 350 miles so was only effective in the Ruhr area, but to
be able to fix a position 350 miles away and, on return, locate
the airfield without the problems experienced in the past was
beyond the wildest dreams of navigators. Its Achilles Heel, like
its earlier German counterpart, *'Knickebein',* was that it was
susceptible to jamming by the enemy. With better navigation and
some more aircraft (i), the saturation raids such as Cologne in
May, 1942, were now possible. For the moment it was effective
until August, when the Germans introduced a countermeasure.

In the meantime Gibson had settled into his first command.
Many people who served with 106 at the time remembered him
well. Selina Richardson served in the WAAFs and was a
wireless operator in the control tower at Coningsby. The first
time she saw Gibson her opinion was that he was a very
handsome man, always smiling and always with his dog, Nigger.
As she got to know Gibson it became the norm for Nigger to
stay with her when Guy was flying. During the early hours of
the morning the ships biscuits, which were sometimes substituted
for bread, kept Nigger going until his master returned. When
Gibson did return he would call up the stairs of the control room
for Nigger and the dog would go to join him, and Guy would
thank her for looking after the dog for him. She remembered an
occasion when in the swimming pool Guy saying to her 'Come

on Selina, my dog does better than that!'

Bert Wigglesworth remembered Gibson visiting him in the sick-bay after a flare had exploded in his hand. Somehow he had found out that Bert was to be married in two weeks and when he left to go on leave Guy presented him with a beautiful set of silver fish servers in a case, with a card expressing his best wishes on the day. He had gone into Boston and bought it himself. Needless to say, Bert has this still today and the set is one of his prized possessions. He also made a point of getting in touch with Bert before he left to join 617 Squadron and the epic dams raid.

Mr Rudd was a mechanic with 106 Squadron and remembers Guy being a very active and amicable CO, but also very young, which, at only 24, he was. Despite his comparative youth, Gibson made every effort to enhance his squadron's offensive fit-for-role, which included constant visits to encourage the workshops who were involved in getting the aircraft airworthy, *'Keep Them Flying At All Costs'* was the groundcrew motto. He also set up a pre-working-day school of navigation to prepare airmen who had been selected for aircrew training, but who were still awaiting their postings. Their extra-curricular classes began at 07.30 hrs until 08.30 hrs each day when their official duties began. It has to be said that on the whole it was not very popular with the student aircrew at the time but later, when they arrived for air crew training, they were glad to have had that initial grounding.

In June 1942, the Lancasters came to 106 Squadron like a breath of fresh air, flown into Coningsby by A.T.A (Air Transport Auxiliary) pilots, many of whom were women. Along with the new bombers came the formidable new 8,000 pound 'Blockbuster' bombs; the bomb doors of the new aircraft being modified to take the new weapon. F/Lt John Hopgood had put in 10 hours on Lancasters with 44 Squadron and was able to show Gibson the ropes. His first operation flying the Lancaster was on 8th July 1942 and on this trip he took a new pilot, P/O

David Shannon, an Australian, who acted as his flight engineer and second pilot. His aircraft on this trip was R5681 and ten aircraft were detailed to bomb the docks at Wilhemshaven. In his log book he details that they bombed from 10,000 feet with five 2000lb bombs and described it as a *'Good Prang'*. He recorded the yards being hit in his log book and there were also hits on the docks. Only one aircraft was missing, Lancaster R5861 of 106 flown by P/O Broderick.

It was a common practice in 106 Squadron to name the aircraft and Gibson chose *Admiral Prune* (his regular Beaufighter whilst with 29 Squadron was *Admiral Foobang III*). On the side of the aircraft W4118-Y was the Walt Disney theme carrying a Mickey Mouse figure with bombs underneath, depicting the number of trips or operations the aircraft had carried out.

The next operation was on 11/12th July, *Operation Barnacle*, to Danzig (now Gdansk) to bomb a submarine works, a distance of 1500 miles. His crew then was P/O Vivian, P/O Ruskell, Sgt Jordan, Sgt Combie and P/O Wickins, plus again P/O Shannon. The operation was carried out at low level and, to spread the German nightfighter cover as thinly as possible, the group split up over the North Sea and flew on independently. Gibson reported missing a ship in the harbour at Danzig (Gdynia) by only 20 yards from 1,000 feet, which subsequently turned out to be an 800 ton flak ship.

On 18th July it was back to the Ruhr and Essen. Out of ten aircraft detailed, only three were able to bomb successfully by the use of Gee. The remainder, including Gibson, were recalled and jettisoned their bombs in the sea.

On 20th July a Bomber Command Directive detailed the target as the Schneider Works at Le Creusot and the Citroen Works in Paris. On 25th July Gibson flew to Horsham St Faith to pick up the Secretary of State for Air, Sir Archibald Sinclair, Air Commodore Clarke and Group Captain Sir Looie Grieg to visit a *'crack station'* as Gibson expressed it.

The 26/27th July saw them with a tough nut to crack, Hamburg. Heavy fires were started but the flak was intense as had been expected. Some 403 aircraft were despatched and Gibson and his crew returned unscathed. Four days later, on the night of the 31st, they undertook the last mission for July, a bombing run to Düsseldorf and again returned unscathed. On 8/9th August it was back to sea, mining *'Silverthorn'* (code name for the Baltic), at Skaw, where, in bad weather conditions, he dropped five mines at 20 second intervals; the purpose was to try and catch the German capital ship *Prince Eugen* if it attempted to break out into the Atlantic.

An agreement between the Air Ministry and the Admiralty had been reached on 25th March 1942, that Bomber Command would lay an average of 1,000 mines per month, provided it did not detract or reduce the main bombing offensive. In 1941, only 1,055 mines were laid and in 1942 this rose to 9,574, representing 14.7 percent of the total sorties carried out by Bomber Command. It was, therefore, a regular part of many squadrons' work and 106 was no exception. On 10th August Gibson and his crew were once again mining, *'Asparagus'* in the Baltic at Helskow where five mines were dropped. On 12/13th August, it was back to *The Reich* when 138 aircraft attacked Mainz. Gibson bombed from 5,000 feet, which was under the cloud base, and dropped 5 x 2000lbs bombs. The raid was an outstanding success with 135 acres of the centre of the town being destroyed. It was also Gibson's 24th birthday.

On 27th August, 9 aircraft of 106 Squadron, armed with a special new bomb designed for attacking ships, headed out towards northern Germany. The target was the German aircraft carrier *Graf Zeppelin*, which was never commissioned, and other naval vessels at the port of Gdynia. The bomb, known as *'The Capital Ship Bomb'* looked like a turnip. Gibson made 12 runs on the German ship *Gneisenau*, finally dropping 6 x 1000lb bombs from 8,000 feet, but missed by 100 feet, not a lot but enough when the target is a ship. His bomb-aimer was a S/L

Richardson, a bombing instructor at Coningsby, it was the first time he had dropped bombs 'in anger' since World War I.

Targets came and went, Saarluten[1] on 1st September, Bremen on the 13th and the Dornier factory at Wismar on the 23rd, in rain and with very poor visibility. On 1st October, 106 Squadron moved to Syerston and on the 9th began low level formation training led by the Station Commander at Syerston, the English Rugby International, Group Captain 'Gus' Walker DSO DFC. Walker's idea of low flying was ground-zero and his uncompromising training schedule and demands on the crews were later to serve Gibson well. On 10th October 95 Lancasters flew in low level formation; there was obviously something in the wind, something which had to be attacked from low level and, naturally, the speculation amongst the crews was rife. This was repeated again on the 11th, this time with 85 Lancasters in a bombing run on Bassingham; Gibson recorded hitting the target pin.

On 15th October, the target was an old chestnut, Cologne. It was not a successful raid by any means owing to the forecast wind being substantially incorrect, resulting in a very scattered bombing pattern. Gibson was flying Lancaster W4118, *Admiral Prune*, which was hit by flak. On the 17th, the reason behind the low flying exercises was revealed, *Operation Robinson*. Nine squadrons of 5 Group were detailed, 94 Lancasters in all, and the target was the Schneider armaments works at Le Creusot, a factory very much on the lines as Krupps in Essen; making guns, tanks and even railway locos. As part of the Op. one formation of six aircraft was to be detached from the main force to attack the Henri Paul transformer and switching station about 5 miles from Le Creusot, Gibson and his crew being one of those allocated to this task. The idea behind it was to cut off

---

[1] - *Saarluten was bombed in error after the Pathfinders marked the wrong target.*

electric power to the Schneider works, and other industrial plants in the area. It was to be a daylight operation and had to be very carefully planned. Nearly 100 aircraft had only seven minutes to get in, bomb and get out between 18.09 hrs and 18.16 hrs. The timing was designed to give them good light to bomb and the cover of darkness for the return.

The daylight run took the Germans by surprise, but without dark for the return trip enemy fighters could have been waiting for them. The 'hedge-hopping' flying for which they had trained so hard was to be used to get them there. Even a thirty-ton bomber, when flying at zero feet, would arrive without warning and, just as rapidly, disappear again. People in France hardly knew the Lancasters, flying close in formation, were overhead until they were well away again. It is also difficult to give a very accurate fix on the direction of the aircraft when they are out of sight so quickly.

The main problem with the 'hedge-hopping' flying is the extreme fatigue for the crew. The pilots have to apply absolute concentration and it is very hard work for the navigators, obtaining crucial fixes simply by visual means when landmarks flashed past in seconds. It was also a completely different form of navigation to that which they were accustomed. Their training and experience had been in accurately finding their way in the darkness and at a great height, not hurtling across the French countryside looking *up* at some of their reference points! It's true that the 'hedge-hopping' technique had been practised in the UK but was a very different matter when flying over unfamiliar country. Special maps were prepared from the coast of France to Le Creusot and at frequent intervals on the map were clearly printed the number of miles still to go before the target was reached. This enabled the navigator and pilot to know if they were keeping exactly to the time-table or not.

The pilot of the first Lancaster to arrive at the target, Wg Cdr Slee, of 49 Squadron, with his navigator P/O Grant, wished to circle the target after bombing but dared not. So many bombers were sweeping into attack and out again there was no margin for error. In the allotted seven minutes 140 tons of bombs were dropped on the Schneider works and huge fires broke out. In the meantime Gibson led the six aircraft that had broken off to attack the transformer station and destroyed it to such an extent that it took two years to repair. Gibson recorded machine gunning the transformer plant from 150 feet and that they sustained damage from the blast of their own bombs; his gunners, together with those of Hopgood's aircraft, recorded firing over 1,000 rounds of machine gun ammunition as well.

On the 22nd the target was Genoa which coincided with the start of the offensive against El Alamein in North Africa. The area was the docks in Genoa where units of the Italian fleet were sheltering. Gibson described it as another *'Good Prang'* and landed at Branston on return after a 9 hour 30 minute trip. He flew the next day from Branston to Chevreston for breakfast and then on to Syerston. On one occasion, during this period, Mr Rudd was due to be interviewed by Gibson for consideration, as he described, for promotion to the dizzy heights of corporal. During the interview he was asked who wrote *'If I shall die'*, which, of course had nothing to do with his job of being promoted to corporal. He could not remember but as soon as he got into the corridor outside it came back to him; it was the first line of a Kipling poem, but by then it was too late. He only recalled seeing Gibson 'blow his top' on one occasion. He had decided to take one of the 'Pot Belly' Lancasters, so-called because of the bomb doors modified to accommodate the 8,000lb 'Blockbusters' bomb, W-Willie instead of his usual kite. However, the 'George' (automatic pilot) was u/s on Willie, and Gibson apparently stood there in shirt sleeves and parachute harness dangling down, threatening the sweating instrument basher with all manner of punishments if the automatic pilot was not ready for take off. Mr Rudd's clear impression is that although Gibson was short in stature he still stood out in a crowd. He said Gibson's uniform was not made to fit him - he fitted the uniform and was a credit to it.

Another example of Gibson's unusual methods is reported as follows: on one occasion when the crews were on their way to briefing, Aussies, Canadians and so on, mainly navigators with maps stuck in their boots and carrying thermos flasks were moving along, chatting amiably, when Gibson's car came up behind them. The car had been fitted with a tannoy-type system which suddenly boomed out with Gibson's voice "Double, you men, double up!" It was repeated and the car pressed ever closer until they started to get a gallop on. Perhaps he felt that discipline was slacking and if this attitude transferred into the air it could cost lives.

The next operation, code name *'Gudgeon'*, was to Milan on the 24th. Once over Milan, Gibson descended to 4,000 feet to identify the target and then bombed it from 5,000 feet. He described it as a marvellous trip with scenery being magnificent over the Alps. On 30th October 1942, Gibson was recommended for the DSO by the station commander at Syerston, Gp Capt 'Gus' Walker. In his recommendation it mentioned his two previous tours of operations and the attacks on Le Creusot in which he had bombed and machine gunned the power station from 500 feet; the raid on Genoa on 22nd October, when he brought back a photograph showing ground detail within two miles of the aiming point; the 24th October when he brought back a series of photographs showing details of the town of Milan; the raids on 11th July, against Danzig and the attack on the warships at Gdynia on 27th August, when he made no less than twelve runs over the target in an endeavour to achieve a successful bombing run. This was endorsed by the then AOC of No 5 Group, AVM Coyton, on the 31st in which he said that Gibson had set a magnificent example to all members of his squadron, and he strongly recommended an immediate DSO. This was gazetted on 20th November 1942.

On 6th November the target was Genoa, which he described as the most concentrated raid he had ever seen. On return he landed at his old fighter base West Malling. On 8th November came *'Operation Husky'*, the invasion by the allies of North Africa. Attacks were made to try and divert the Italian Fleet from interfering with the landings. On the 18th came another Italian target - Turin and the Fiat works which he bombed from 6,000 feet, landing at Middle Wallop on return. On 21st November came a new Bomber Command Directive, the Destruction of Towns and of the ball-bearing factory at Schweinfurt.

On the 28th, Turin once again, and every bomb seemed to go in the right place. Gibson described it as another *'Good prang'* and bombed from 7,000 feet, taking cine-film of the attack, one of his hobbies. In his crew he carried Major Mullock, of the Royal Artillery, who was the Bomber Command Flak liaison officer. On 2nd December came another Bomber Command Directive. The primary targets were to be in Northern Italy to create serious disruption and affect production.

In the log book of the station commander at Syerston, 'Gus' Walker, himself became an entry for 8th December 1942. Thirty aircraft were taxying around the perimeter waiting for the green light to take off, the target was Turin. At the time Gus was in the flying control tower with Gibson when, all of a sudden, it was noticed that some incendiaries had dropped out of the bomb door of a reserve aircraft being bombed up on the far side of the field. Gus immediately raced over in his car, along with the fire tender, and Gibson had to stay in the control tower, being the next senior officer to Gus. He saw Gus get out of his car and run towards the aircraft and get into it. Once inside he apparently saw that the incendiaries were in fact cooking the bomb they had fallen on and it was only a matter of time before the lot went up. Running from the aircraft he warned the fire crew to get clear. When it did go off, a 4,000 pounder, Gus was still only about twenty yards from the aircraft. A pall of smoke went up into the air for some 2,000 feet and Gus was blown about 200 yards and a chunk of jagged metal took off his right arm just above the elbow.

A mobile surgical unit was sent from Rauceby under the command of F/Lt Braithwaite, who gave Gus a blood transfusion on the way to the hospital. LAC Hughes had also been hurt badly by pieces of metal in the legs and went in the ambulance with Gus. Besides losing his arm Gus had lost a considerable amount of blood and was severely shocked. Four other airmen were injured, and one, AC2 Thwaite died of his injuries on 11th December. Before being removed to hospital Gus asked Guy if he would look for his arm as it had a brand new glove on it! He also asked him to phone the AOC and ask him if he would take on a one armed station commander in two months time. Relinquishing command of RAF Syerston on admittance to hospital at Rauceby, it was Gibson who took over temporary command of the station.

John Wilson remembers Guy Gibson as seeming to be older than most of the aircrew, the average age of whom was 19. John, from Canada, was himself only twenty at the time. John clearly remembers Gibson's dedication to the job in hand and to his men. He never expected or asked for more from his crews than he himself was willing to give and do. It was no secret that he regarded pilots in a class well above all other aircrew regardless of rank. Some crew members were, apparently, mildly offended by this attitude. In fairness it has to be said that in John's view Gibson was not universally loved by all his crews, but he certainly was respected.

Another squadron member, Mr Holder, saw the wrath of Gibson on one occasion. On a 'stand down' day after three consecutive nights of operations there would normally be time to catch up with one or two things that had been left, to write some letters home, etc. But the ground crews had to wait for the CO (Gibson) to make his inspection of the flights before they could fall out. On this occasion he had his wife, Eve, with him who was known, as Mr Holder remembers, as *'The Pocket Venus'*. *'Gibbo'* suddenly blew his top, someone had been smoking in his aircraft, but oddly enough the five groundcrew who looked after it were all non-smokers.

On another occasion they were having problems with Gibson's aircraft before take off and panic was setting in. The problem was loss of air pressure in the brakes. The groundcrew jumped on a tractor with their tool bags, air bottles and began running through the possible causes before they even got to the bomber. It was vital that the brake pressure was right, particularly on take off, when the brakes were fully applied as the engines were opened up to full boost. When the whole aircraft was shuddering under the full power of the four Merlin engines the brakes would be released and the aircraft accelerated immediately, rather than beginning its take off run as the power was increased.

As was usual the groundcrew did their job and Gibson took off, they then settled down to wait for his return. Because Gibson's aircraft had taken off after a brake fault had been fixed but not completely tested the crew were under orders to stop Gibson's aircraft, on its return, after it had left the runway and tow it to the dispersal point. This had a slope called 'The Graveyard', the reason being that if the brakes were faulty the aircraft would run down the slope and into a field. The aircraft returned and they flashed their torches to Gibson for him to stop, but he had other ideas about that and roared on scattering everyone before him and parked up at dispersal.

At this point it was Mr Holder's job to present the aircraft's captain with the Form 700, known in the RAF as the 'Bible'. It was the aircraft's log sheets and on them the aircrew would enter any faults that had occurred so that the groundcrew could put them right. Suddenly the door at the rear of the Lancaster burst open and to quote Mr Holder, '... to say Gibson was upset would be putting it mildly!' He apparently pointed at Mr Holder and said to the duty officer 'Put this man on a charge, he's drunk!' It was 05.00 hrs in the morning, to make sure his orders had been carried out he 'phoned up at 08.30 hrs. As it was

Holder did not drink at all and this was common knowledge. Despite this Mr Holder remembered Gibson with affection saying, 'My CO, *'Gibbo'*, yes, you could say he was some 'Guy'!'

14 - 106 Squadron 42/43. Gibson's crew: Rushell, Wickens, Gibson, McGregor, Muttrie, Oliver.

In 1943 came the start of the 'Bomber Offensive', which was to continue right to the end of the war, ever increasing and with ever more demands made on the crews. The Americans by daylight, playing their part, choosing the town of Wilhemshaven for their first strike on 27th January 1943. The Casablanca Conference supported the bombing policy:

> 'The basic mission of the strategic air force is the progressive destruction and dislocation of the German military, industrial and economic system to a point where his capability for any resistance is fatally weakened.'

On 17/18th January 1943, Gibson took off at 16.35 hrs heading for Berlin, his load a single 8,000lb bomb. His aircraft for this operation was R5611-W; W4118-Y, *'Admiral Prune'* was flown by S/L John Searby. As well as his normal crew Gibson had on board Major Richard Dimbleby, a war correspondent. The bomb aimer was Sub-Lieutenant Mutrie, of the Fleet Air Arm, seconded to Bomber Command to help with ship recognition. He'd become bored with that and had managed to get on a few operations with 106 (he was later to go missing on a trip to Stuttgart when his aircraft crashed at Amiens and he was thrown through the roof of the aircraft and killed). Others in the crew were Pilot Officer Rushell, Flight Sergeant Lewis, Pilot Officer Wickens, Pilot Officer Hutchison and Flight Lieutenant Oliver.

Brian Oliver was an ex-policeman and recalled that his wireless operator, 'Hutch' Hutchison, once said he always kept his curtain drawn so as not to see the bursting flak. This, he maintained, enabled him to concentrate better on his radio set, particularly when over the target. He also suffered greatly from air sickness but never let that stand in the way of being in on an Op. 'Hutch' was totally dedicated to doing his job well and it was easy to see why Gibson later selected him to go to 617 Squadron with him. The radio communications and training for the dams raid was vital and there was no one better equipped than 'Hutch' to deal with this side of the raid. But that, as yet, was still some way away.

They took off safely, although heavily laden, and were soon climbing over Syerston. Dimbleby looked out of the window and saw at least 40 Lancasters climbing alongside and recorded that they seemed to be *'suspended in the air'*. They then passed over the coast and into occupied territory. Up came the puffs of smoke from the flak but with nothing audible because of the constant roar of the aircraft's engines. Up front Gibson sat up high in his pilot's seat pulling and pushing his bomber about, 'as if it were a toy', as Dimbleby described it. It was after they had climbed and gone on oxygen that Dimbleby suddenly dropped off into a doze. When he awoke he was sitting on the floor with Sgt McGregor, the flight engineer, next to him. As McGregor pushed him upright Gibson saw what was happening and asked, 'What's up?' 'Nipped his oxygen tube' replied Jock McGregor. At which Gibson advised Dimbleby 'Want to watch that. Keep it under your arm and away from the parachute harness.'

Richard Dimbleby's recording of the approach and bombing run over Berlin was one of the most notable of the war. It graphically recorded the stark call, 'Berlin' over the intercom which alerted everyone to the imminence of the target. Then came the ring of searchlights and the intense flak bursts in dirty yellow clusters, one explosion lifting the aircraft as the shell burst. As the incendiaries went down the area below became silver and the fires turned to a dull red. Gibson told Dimbleby that when he reached the target he was, 'as cold as ice' and knew exactly what he was doing, he also told him to get his cine camera ready. Dimbleby described the target incendiaries dropping like a magic carpet of glittering jewels which lay like a giant cobweb. The target area was the Alexanderplatz Station and Gibson's voice cut in on the intercom, short and to the point, 'I am going in to bomb' and the aircraft headed straight for the raging inferno below. Then a shell burst just feet away and Dimbleby lost his footing, hitting his head on the instrument panel. Settling onto the bombing run is always the most dangerous time as it is necessary to fly straight and level, easy prey for the gunners. Dimbleby was apparently sick on the floor and kept his head down until he heard 'Bombs Gone'. It was an encouraging thought that somewhere far below them Hitler and his gang could be hiding in a shelter and there was always the million-to-one chance of a direct hit!

The trip home was uneventful, no contact being made with nightfighters. When they arrived back at Syerston it was one hour and twenty minutes before they could land because of the stacking system used to bring returning aircraft in. When they finally did land at 01.50 hrs Dimbleby said, 'I wouldn't have missed it for the world' It was the first time a war correspondent had reported after being on an operation over Germany and that day he went straight back to London and gave a broadcast on the radio. The Air Ministry were delighted and Bomber Command sent a telegram commending the good work. Dimbleby was to fly on no less than 20 operations with the RAF. He wrote to Gibson later and said, 'I was paralysed with fright, but it was an unforgettable experience.' Part of transcript of his broadcast went as follows:

> 'This they do as a regular routine job which is hard, tiring and dangerous. *'Per Adua Ad Astra'* is the motto of the RAF, which translated means 'Through Hardship To The Stars' I now understand the hardship and I am pleased to have seen the stars with them.'

Gibson described it as a 'Good Trip and fairly successful. The residents got it.' The flying time was logged as 9 hours and 15 minutes. Logistically the trip was not that successful, the force composed of 170 Lancasters and 17 Halifax found the target more or less obscured by cloud, although a good number of bombs, including the 8,000 pounders fell on Berlin. The aero engine plant at Spandau was damaged and the losses were recorded as 'slight'. Twenty-two bombers out of the 187 despatched were unaccounted for. Eight of the nine bombers dispatched from 106 Squadron were able to make an attack. Gibson reported making three runs on the target before bombing from 18,000 feet. S/L Searby reported Berlin to be swamped but spoilt by cloud, F/Lt Hopgood bombed from 18,500 and his bombs dropped in the target area supported by a bombing photograph.

The aircraft *'Admiral Prune'* W4118-Y, shared by Gibson and

Searby was later lost on 5th February 1943 on a raid to Turin. At the time it had logged 340 flying hours. Gibson's aircraft on the Berlin raid, R5611-W, went missing on 14th May 1943, during the 'Battle of the Ruhr.' At the time the target was Bochum and it had recorded some 239 hours on its F 700.

15 - Early 1943. (l to r) S/L Searby, W/Cdr Gibson, S/L Ward-Hunt. In the background is 'Admiral Prune' which was later lost.

On 14th January 1943, the Bomber Command Directive gave the targets as Lorient, St Nazaire, Brest, and La Pallice - in that order. The priority at this time was U-Boats, and their destruction. Three days later, on the 17th, it changed again. Attacks on industrial centres in Northern Italy-Milan, Turin, Genoa, and if possible Spezia were to be priority, but without prejudicing attacks on Berlin. Harris, at this time, was under pressure from Churchill who, in turn, was under pressure from Stalin who wanted attacks on Berlin as there had been none in 1942. On 4th February the Directive was once again changed: attacks on submarine construction yards, German aircraft factories, transportation, oil plants and other significant targets in the enemy war industry. Berlin was still mentioned whenever conditions were suitable, to rock the enemy's morale, or at least to placate the Russians and help raise Soviet morale.

Gibson's next trip was back to Italy and Milan on 14th February. He described it as a good trip getting six aiming points. He took F/Lt Morrison as his second pilot for flight experience or *'First Dickie Trip'*. One crew of 101 Sqdn were awarded no less than six Conspicuous Gallantry Medals and one Distinguished Service Order[2] after being attacked by an Italian CR42 fighter. Gibson took about 20 minutes cine film on this trip and also brought back a bombing photograph from 11,000 feet.

On the 25th, the target was Nuremberg, the weather was bad and the Pathfinders were late in marking, necessitating the main force hanging around in the target area too long, which was not to be encouraged. There was little respite as the offensive gained momentum and on the 26th, the target was Köln (Cologne), Gibson's 169th operational flight, and 70th bomber operation in which he recorded huge fires.

On one night the famous Lew Stone Big Band came to Syerston, bringing the soprano, Millicent Phillips, along. Gibson and a number of the 106 officers were sitting in the front row. After about 30 minutes six or seven 106 NCO aircrew came in via a door near the stage and shortly after Lew Stone and Millicent Phillips were seen to be looking through the joins in the floor boards. Gibson was sitting there grinning, apparently a cat had been put under the stage and its meowing was disturbing the concert.

When 'Gee' came to 106 Squadron a few navigators were sent on a course and then they, in turn, would train the remainder.

---

[2] - *It is interesting to note that P/O FW Gates, who was the only officer in the crew, was awarded the DSO although he was the Wop/AG (wireless operator/gunner) and not the pilot.*

At the course briefing, S/L Scrivenor mentioned that if the aircraft was in trouble the instruction was to push the governor switch to destroy the 'Gee' box which was still 'Secret'. F/Lt Danny Walker, David Shannon's navigator, told Gibson's navigator, Frank Rushell, that he did not know where this switch was in the aircraft and Rushell agreed to show him. They climbed into the aircraft and Frank, in showing him where it was, pressed it and blew up the Gee box. Needless to say Gibson was not impressed, but did not hold a grudge. The fact was that Rushell had not known that part of the aircraft's circuit was 'live' at the time.

16 - Gibson with 106 Squadron at Syerston 1942 (Imperial War Museum).

The secret of Gibson's success as a CO was in his ability to select good flight commanders, he had S/L 'Dim' de Lacey-Woolridge, a former BBC producer, as 'B' Flight Commander. He had the ability to put across the briefing in a humorous way, not easy when you are sending men out to be killed. His briefings went on the lines 'We'll set course for home from the column of smoke' etc, S/L Stenner was another gem as a flight commander. S/L John Searby (later Group Captain and was to lead the raid on Peenemunde) remembers Guy writing in a blue exercise book, which later was to become 'Enemy Coast Ahead' which he wrote in 1944 and was published in 1946. He said that with Guy you made briefing and take off time on the button and to the minute. Gibson's name, as John remembers, was always first on the operational order. His style was to lead from the front and his men respected him for it.

17 - 106 Squadron, Syerston, Gibson with crew (l to r): (?) possibly Sgt. Pegler, Hutchison (later 617) Gibson, Rushell, Oliver, Wickens.

It was 11th March 1943 before he was to fly again, this time to Stuttgart. It was to be his last flight with 106 Squadron and the last that tour. The 'Battle of the Ruhr' had started six days before with a raid on Essen, and was to continue until July 1943 with 25 raids on Ruhr towns and cities. The Stuttgart raid was not a successful operation, the Pathfinders had done their job on this occasion, but the main force was late. The Germans were also using dummy incendiaries for the first time and many of the bombs landed in open country south west of the town. Outbound Gibson was thinking about his overdue leave and how he'd spend it relaxing in Cornwall and playing with Nigger, a long way from bombing operations. Suddenly, his port outboard engine was hit by flak and stopped, posing him with a real dilemma. If he aborted and turned back he would have to do another operation to complete his tour. He conferred with his navigator, F/Lt Scrivenor, and they decided they would lose height to 4000 feet and try to climb to bombing height when they arrived over Stuttgart. They managed to do this and after successfully dropping their bombs headed for home, and leave, or so he thought.

18 - Hutchison with Gibson. 'Hutch' was to be requested by Gibson to join 617 Squadron (Imperial War Museum).

19 - Towards the end of their time at Syerston - Gibson and Nigger with various aircrew.

On this trip he had as second pilot P/O Walter Thompson, a Canadian who had only that day arrived on 106 Squadron. He later recalled in his own book that the aircraft was ED649 X-Ray, and that as he remembers it was the starboard outer engine that was hit and not the port as Gibson had recorded. Gibson had asked Thompson to take over for a while on the return trip as his leg was painful from continually holding the rudder bar hard over to counter the unequal thrust of two engines on one wing, even with full trim. However, he took over again for the landing at Syerston.

The next day an official 106 Squadron photograph was taken before Gibson's departure. Before leaving he gave a farewell speech in front of the flight officers at Syerston, but on this occasion the intercom or microphone, which had been hastily fitted, let him down. After much tinkering without result, his patience gave out and he quickly said 'I thank all you chaps for the jobs that you have done for me - especially this one!' he of course meant the microphone. With a quick tug on the mike he turned and walked away.

On the 12th he was recommended for a bar to his DSO and this showed 172 sorties and 642.30 operational flying hours in his log book. It was endorsed by the AOC of No 5 Group, AVM The Rt Hon Ralph Cochrane, on the 17 March, and on the 20th by ACM Sir Arthur Harris who said:

> 'Any Captain who completes 172 sorties in outstanding manner is worth 2 DSO's, if not the VC. Bar to the DSO approved.'

This was gazetted on 2nd April, 1943. He now had two DSO's to add to his two DFC's. Gibson was posted to HQ No 5 Group on 15th March, where he was asked by AVM Cochrane if he would do one more trip. 'Yes' was his unequivocal reply and he was prepared to leave it at that, even though he was not told what this trip was or what it would entail. He himself thought it was the 'Tirpitz' and was to become more and more convinced of this as the training and organisation of the operation progressed. After all, who would have possibly guessed that they could burst a huge dam with a bomb that bounced!

On 24th March 1943, he was posted to command 'X' Squadron. The only member of his crew to follow him was F/Lt 'Hutch' Hutchison, who hailed from Liverpool.

RECOMMENDATION FOR IMMEDIATE AWARD.

~~RECOMMENDATION FOR HONOURS AND AWARDS.~~

Christian Names... GUY PENROSE .... Surname... GIBSON, D.S.O., D.F.C. & Bar.

Rank... Squadron Leader (Acting Wing Commander).. Official Number... 39438

Command or Group... No. 5 Group, Bomber Command. Unit... No. 106 Squadron.

Total hours flown on operations.
1. 1st Tour (Hampdens) 242.30
2. 2nd Tour (Fighters) 199.45
3. 3rd Tour (Lancasters) 200.44

Number of Sorties... 172

Total hours flown on operations since receipt of previous award... 65.54

Number of sorties since receipt of previous award... 9

Recognition for which recommended... Bar to D.S.O.

Appointment held... Officer Commanding No. 106 (B) Squadron.

Particulars of meritorious service for which the recommendation is made.

W/Cdr. Gibson has now completed three operational tours, two in Bomber and one in Fighter Command. In his last tour he has distinguished himself particularly by inspiring leadership and unwavering determination that each and every crew in his Squadron must hit the target.

In the past two months he has taken part in six sorties on BERLIN, ESSEN, COLOGNE, MILAN, NUREMBURG and STUTTGART at times when his personal example and readiness to share the hazards would and did make a substantial contribution to morale in his Squadron.

On his last sortie on STUTTGART on 11/12 March 1943 one of his engines would not give the necessary power to enable him to follow the prearranged flight plan and he was faced with the alternatives of an early return or a low attack. W/Cdr. Gibson unhesitatingly chose the low attack to provide convincing proof of the tactical policy which he had so consistently advocated in his Squadron. He carried out his attack successfully and brought back an excellent recco report.

For such determined and gallant leadership W/Cdr. Gibson is strongly recommended for the award of a bar to the D.S.O.

GROUP CAPTAIN, COMMANDING
R.A.F. STATION, SYERSTON.

Date... 14. 3. 43...

Remarks by Air or other Officer Commanding

Wing Commander Gibson has now handed over command of 106 Squadron after an outstandingly successful tour as Squadron Commander. In view, however, of the recent award of the Distinguished Service Order I recommend that he should now be considered for the award of a Second Bar to his Distinguished Flying Cross rather than to the Distinguished Service Order.

Date... 17th March 1943... Rank... A/V/M ... A.V.M. A.O.C.

Any Captain who completes 172 sorties in succession is worth 2 DSOs if not a V.C. Passed so approved
A.H.T.
2c/3

84

CHAPTER SIX

'X' SQUADRON

Seven weeks of breathless preparation and intense training were the prelude to the war's greatest air attack. A successful outcome would be the destruction of the Möhne and Eder Dams and the consequent flooding of a wide stretch of Germany's Ruhr Industry.

Dr Barnes Wallis believed that, at least in theory, the Ruhr Dams were military targets whose destruction would deprive the Germans of water (the production of one ton of steel required 100 tons of water) and electrical power to the industrial area. In 1938 various targets had been discussed by the Air Ministry Bombing Committee in the event of war with Germany. The dams, situated in West Westphalia, were discussed on 26th July 1938, the object of their destruction being the cutting off of supplies of water for industrial and domestic use and the causing of flooding and subsequent wide-spread damage to industrial plants, railways, and waterways. The dams themselves had been constructed as regulating measures in the area to stop the natural flooding and near-drought conditions which came and went with the seasons. They had not actually been constructed to generate hydro-electric power, that was just a bonus.

The main dams, of about twelve in Germany, were the Möhne, Eder, Sorpe, Ennepe, and Lister - the Möhne, Eder and Sorpe being the most important of all in the Westphalia area. Wallis remembered from history that the naval gunners in the eighteenth and nineteenth centuries had deliberately bounced cannon balls off the sea to extend the range of thier guns. So, Wallis thought, why not a bomb that would do exactly the same thing? The dams were protected by a dual screen of torpedo netting suspended from large steel buoys, preventing any form of underwater attack. Any form of torpedo-like projectile was out of the question but the possibility of a 'bouncing' or 'skipping' bomb occurred to Wallis. Based on this, experiments were initiated using models of dams with encouraging results.

With the Lancaster entering service in 1942, and better bombing techniques, things started to look more feasible. Tests were undertaken at Teddington Water Tanks, trying to establish a scientifically predictable pattern of bounces and back-spin[1] for the radically new bomb. When the time came for a full-scale test, government backing was required. The first tests were made at Chesil Beach near Weymouth, Dorset, using a Wellington bomber flown by Mutt Summers (whom Gibson had first approached about being a pilot). The bomb aimer for the occasion was Barnes Wallis himself (he had also designed the Wellington Bomber). The first few tests were a disappointment, the bomb breaking up when it hit the water, but after the casing had been strengthened it worked.

By February 1943, the bomb had been given the code-name *'Upkeep'* and Sir Arthur Harris, as C-in-C of Bomber Command, was approached. However, having been shown so many inventions that would *'shorten the war'* he was not convinced about a bomb that would bounce on water. In fact he called it 'Tripe!' His main concern, having fought so hard for them, was what he considered as the unacceptable risk of losing Lancasters and their crews. Notwithstanding that Harris agreed, on 22nd February 1943, to see the film that had been made of the bomb drops. There is little doubt that this was only possible because it was arranged by Mutt Summers, who knew Harris.

After seeing the film Harris showed interest and said he would think about it. The next day, however, Wallis received what to him was a bomb-shell - the dams project was off! He promptly resigned, which caused Churchill himself to become directly involved and was given the *'Upkeep'* papers. After reading the

---

[1] - *The back-spin was an essential part of the operation of the bomb because it caused the bomb to submerge whilst in contact with the dam wall and to remain in contact as it sank to thirty feet.*

report he promptly gave the go-ahead for the operation. By the 26th it was official and anything that Wallis wanted was made available as he continued with his trials.

For Harris it was a case of organising the squadron to carry out the operation and, in turn, brought the AOC of No 5 Group in, as it was his group from which the men would be used to carry out the operation. When Harris asked Cochrane who he wanted to lead the raid he had no hesitation in naming Gibson. So, on 15th March, instead of going on leave to Cornwall, Gibson was told to report to No 5 Group HQ at Grantham. At this stage he knew nothing of the detail of the operation, only that it was *'top secret'* and tagged as a *'Churchill Priority.'* Gibson was asked by Cochrane if he would make one more trip to which he readily agreed, still knowing very little about the operation he was to lead. On the 18th they met again, this time with Group Captain Charles Whitworth, the station commander at Scampton. He himself had, in 1940/41, commanded a bomber squadron and had been awarded the DSO and DFC. At this stage the squadron to undertake the operation was known as 'X'. On 24th March Gibson was posted to Scampton and 'X' squadron became a reality and was designated 617 Squadron RAF.

The next 42 days and nights would result in a legend. The empty No 2 Hangar, which had previously been used by 49 Squadron, was to be the home of 617 Squadron for the weeks ahead. By the time it had been cleaned out ten Lancasters, of which eight were new, had arrived and so began the training from 08.00 hrs to 20.00 hrs each day. The crews, hand-picked for this operation, began to assemble; some came as crews, some as parts of crews and a few individuals, all came together to begin the work-up for the Op. The nucleus of the administration staff came from 57 Sqadron, already based at Scampton. Sgt Jim Heveron, who had been with 57 Squadron since September 1939 and served in France with them (managing to get out at the Dunkirk evacuation), became the Orderly Room Sergeant. He had been attached to Operations at No 5 Group HQ and had been

20 - Sergeant Jim Heveron. Orderly room Sgt. 617 Squadron.

with Gibson there ten days before and was called back off leave for his posting to 617 Squadron.

Jim remembered that when he arrived at No 2 Hangar there were men milling about all over the place and, upstairs in the CO's office, Gibson was looking a trifle bemused. The first adjutant, a WWI man, was with him as well as F/Sgt George 'Chiefy' Powell[2]. Jim and 'Chiefy' knew each other having both served with 57 Sqadron. Although 'Chiefy' was nominated to be the NCO in charge of discipline it was, in fact, Jim who looked after admin matters, releasing 'Chiefy' for other duties.

The adjutant was soon replaced by Harry Humphries, who came from 50 squadron, the engineering officer S/L Clifford Caple always known as 'Capable' Caple came from Group HQ and the armament officer, F/Lt Henry Watson, joined them from 83 Squadron.

Things had settled down quickly in the first week ready for the

---

[2] - *George Powell had joined the RAF in 1928 but transferred to the reserve in 1935 and then re-enlisted in July, 1939. In 1939/40 he flew as an air gunner with 500 Squadron based at Manston then part of Coastal Command until he was posted to 57 Squadron in November 1940. There he stopped flying and became responsible for discipline. He never wore his flying badge or brevet as he felt the aircrew would perhaps take advantage and think of him as just another grounded airman.*

training programme to begin. Gibson was totally immersed in the work-up to the Op and said to Jim 'I'm a flyer, admin is your job.' Flt/Lt Harry Humphries, who had replaced the WWI Adjutant was, like Jim, given a great deal of latitude by Gibson. Most of the time Gibson was flying, which was exactly what he wanted, and told Jim anything he want signed was to be put in front of him and he'd sign it. Apparently Gibson said, 'If you put a piece of toilet paper in front of me I will sign it.' Jim was more than once tempted but did not.

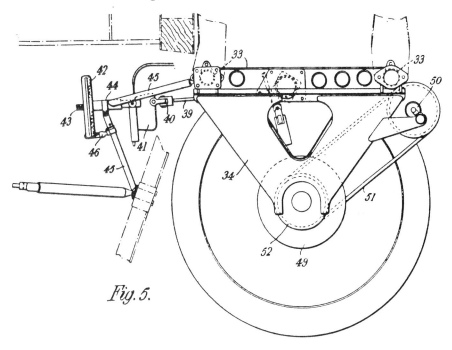

Fig. 5.

Side elevation of the bomb in the housing.
Note the driving mechanism marked (50).

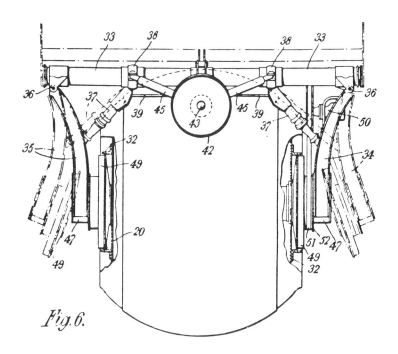

Fig. 6.

*Rear elevation of the bomb showing the securing arms
in place and in the release position.*

Twenty Lancasters were modified to take the new bomb, the weapon was 60 inches long and 50 inches in diameter and had three hydrostatic pistols set to detonate at 30 feet below the water. Each bomb would be fitted with a 90 second time-fuse which was initiated on release, its purpose being to destroy the weapon if the pistols failed to function, or it failed to reach the required depth of 30 feet. Each end of the 3/8" steel cylindrical casing carried a hollow circular track which was 20 inches in diameter into which disc-like wheels mounted on the supporting caliper arms were fitted. The total weight of the weapon was 9,250 lbs, of which 6,600 lbs was charge weight.

The 'store', 'mine', or 'bomb' as it was called by various people was hung up under the Lancaster by means of two V-shaped arms, incorporating as much of the cylindrical bomb inside the bomb-bay as possible. Actual attachment was by means of two disc-like wheels which engaged the cylindrical case of the bomb on either side of its central axis. The securing disks were mounted on ball races set into the load-bearing arms which allowed the bombs to be rotated in situ. Powerful springs acting outwardly ensured the opening of the arms when the release mechanism was actuated. The rotation of the bomb before release was effected by a V.S.G Hydraulic Motor, 15 to 18 inches in height, mounted in the bomb bay just forward of the V-shaped arms. The motor was driven by a hydraulic pump on the port inboard engine and was started by the wireless operator about thirty minutes before arrival at the dams, rotating the bomb at a controlled 500 revs per minute.

The Germans had, of course, had their meetings prior to or in the early stages of the war where the military leadership, as opposed to the politicians, had realistically discussed vulnerable targets within Germany. The dams had been discussed although they had visualised a completely different method of attack on them. They had imagined what they called *'Winterballon'* (winter balloon) which was ingenious enough in its own right but only for use in winter. Their advisors had forseen a time when the lakes behind the dams would be frozen and a special bomb would be dropped to crack through the ice as close as possible to the dam wall and inside the torpedo nets. Then a heavy duty floatation bag would be deployed and inflated, lifting the bomb clear of the bottom, bobbing along under the ice. In this position the bomb would be carried by the flow below the ice to the dam wall. They had speculated that a number of these bombs were to be released at the same time to make sure at least one got through. The bomb would have a long time fuse to allow it time to travel down to the dam before detonating.

Gradually the logistical exercise that guided 617 Squadron towards their, as yet unknown target, moved on. The Lancasters that were to actually undertake the operation began to arrive, having been modified in a hangar at Farnborough, some by Avro

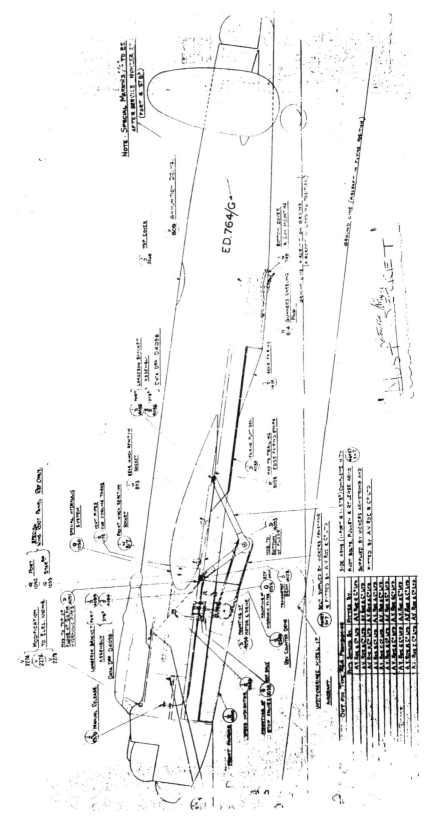

The modification blueprint for the Lancasters, thought to have been destroyed in a fire some years ago. Found in A.V. Roe archives.

and some by Vickers. Jim Heveron remembers the funny looking aircraft being delivered and the new speculation about the target. What was clear was that with the actual delivery of the aircraft the Op. couldn't be far away - things were looking up!

Jim Heveron also remembered examples of Gibson's style of command as being not exactly from the staff college handbook of management but effective nonetheless: on one occasion Gibson said to Jim Heveron that he was going to Group and to leave his flying helmet out for him to pick up for a night training run. Jim in turn gave the order that the office was to be left open, but it was not. When Gibson arrived he found the office locked and Jim had to get the offending airmen to break the glass above the door and climb in and as he was a six-footer it wasn't easy. On another occasion, when an airman spilt ink on the fuselage of Gibson's aircraft, he made him walk two miles to the flight office, get a bucket of water and a brush, walk back, and clean it off. On the other hand, Jim recalled, he was a very understanding CO when making a judgement on summary charges, but an absolute tartar if it was a matter of security or flight safety.

Time, unbeknown to the crews at 617 Squadron, was getting short. All experimentation had indicated that if the water levels were three metres below the crest of the dams the effectiveness of the explosion would be reduced; if it was six metres down there was serious doubt as to whether they could be breached. The reservoirs would be full in May/June after the flood of the melting snows and would fall by three metres a month from then on. A good full moon on the night of the attack was also needed to enable low flying in what was bad terrain around the dams, particularly the Eder Dam.

As far back as February 1943, Bomber Command had requested that a model of the Möhne Dam should be made and a section known as 'W' received an order to make a scale model of 1:6000. At this time the only photographs available had been taken on 4th and 5th of September 1941, but these only covered the area of the dam and not the dam itself. However, from ground photographs and a German 1:2500 map, an enlarged mosaic was prepared and delivered to 'W' section on 12th February. The model was then completed and despatched to Bomber Command on the 17th.

On the 19th, a special sortie was flown from RAF Benson, which succeeded in covering the Möhne Dam. The report, prepared by a Captain Espenhahn of the Army Section, covered the defences around the area and was issued on 21st February, 1943. The Central Intelligence Units (C.I.U) were based at Medmenham and were designated by single letters of the alphabet: 'D', 'R', 'W', and 'V' and were under the control of Wing Commander Kendall. 'D' Section, under Wing Commander Howard Thomas, was responsible for the interpretation of reports; 'R' co-ordinated the demands of those responsible for the planning of operations; 'W' provided the necessary data, such as photographic material and maps at the correct scale for 'V' who produced the scale models of the dams. A second, very detailed report, was completed and with it was a plan drawn up by F/O d'Arcy Smith of 'D' Section, completed on the 27th. The result was that the model itself now required certain modifications, which were completed by 3rd March. On 4th April 1943, a model of the Sorpe Dam was started and completed by the 19th and the model of the Eder Dam was, in fact, only completed on 17th May, the day before the raid.

Gibson had the task of selecting 147 men for the operation, the number required to crew 21 Lancasters, all were to come from No 5 Group. Three of the crews selected came from Gibson's old 106 Squadron and other individuals who were chosen from Gibson's personal experience of them: one was the man who had first shown him the ropes on the Lancaster, F/Lt John Hopgood DFC and Bar with 45 operations under his belt; another was P/O David Shannon DFC, who had flown his first trips with 106 in Gibson's crew, and the third P/O Lewis Burpee, a Canadian married to an English girl and who had been awarded the DFM after 26 operations. Gibson had a great affection for aircrew from the Dominions; Canada, Australia, New Zealand, and the Colonies and this was reflected when it came to the choice of his own crew. He admired them having come so far to fight for the *'Old Country'* and asked the British crews to look after them and, if possible, take them home when they went on leave.

Gibson's crew for the unknown Op., apart from 'Hutch' Hutchison, was a new one: the flight engineer Sgt. John Pulford had only flown 10 operations with 97 Sqdn before joining 617 Squadron; his navigator, F/Lt Harlo Taerum DFC, from Canada, had completed one tour with 50 Squadron; F/O 'Spam' Spafford DFM came from Australia and was to be Gibson's bomb aimer, an important crew position on this operation, so much responsibly lay on him to drop the bomb in the right place, and at the right time. 'Spam' had also flown with 50 Squadron and been awarded an immediate DFM after 15 operations. Gibson's front gunner was to be P/O Deering, another Canadian, but born in Ireland of Scottish parents and the last man was the rear gunner, the ever faithful F/Lt Trevor-Roper. He had started the war in the Army, but had transferred and had 51 operations under his belt, bringing him the DFM back in 1941 when rear gunner to S/L 'Gus' Walker (later Air Commodore, and even later Air Chief Marshal).

S/L Henry Young was to be his 'A' Flight Commander, he was always known as 'Dinghy' having ditched twice and been posted to command a 'Dinghy School' as a joke. The 'B' Flight Commander was S/L Henry Maudsley, described as one of the most outstanding captains in No 5 Group. Many of the other crews were rated amongst the most experienced crews in the Group, but there were also others with very little experience of operations. At one end of the scale there was one man who was on his first operational trip and at the other end there were 17 DFCs, 3 DSOs and 10 DFMs shared between the crews.

The messing was shared with 57 Squadron, who wondered

about a squadron that never went on operations. They, of course, were flying night after night as a main force squadron and all the crews of 617 Squadron could do was grin and bear it; at that stage they did not even know what they were training for. At the end of March, and with most of the air and groundcrews having arrived, Gibson assembled everyone and stood on the bonnet of his car in No 2 hangar at Scampton. He didn't mince his words, telling them that the odds were heavily against them and that if anyone wanted to withdraw he could without any thought of them being labelled cowards or branded LMF (Lack of Moral Fibre). No one withdrew.

The code names had now been set for the operation:

'Upkeep' - the Dams Bomb

'Chastise' - Operation Code-Name

Gibson was very keen to make sure security was kept and there was no idle talk. *'Careless talk costs lives'* was the watchword of the day. He also encouraged the groundcrew to go on the training flights whenever possible, thus strengthening the already existing bonds between ground and air crews. This extended in some unexpected directions when, for example, Peggy Patterson, who was a driver in No 5 Group driving an Austin Shooting Brake, went on one or two of the exercise flights over the Derwent Lakes.

The training, which began on 31st March, was initially to get used to low flying and navigating at zero heights, something in which Gibson was already well practised. Subsequently it was 1st April before Gibson made his first flight. It immediately became clear that judging the height of the aircraft from the water at night was going to be a major problem. The release height was so crucial that it was simply not practical to rely on the standard altimeter. The solution came from Ben Lockspeiser, Director of Scientific Research, who came up with two angled spotlights which cast a light on the water. As the aircraft reduced height and got lower, the light beams came nearer and nearer each other until, finally, they met and became one. The aircraft was then flying at precisely the required height. It was not until 5th April 1943, that Gibson was told of the target. Armed with that knowledge he ordered specialist training using lakes in Yorkshire and Scotland.

The second crucial problem to be overcome was the distance from the dam at which the bombs were to be released. It was vital that this was correct, too close and the bomb would bounce over the dam, too far out and it might not reach it. The solution was a 'Y' shaped piece of plywood with a peep-hole at the bottom of the leg of the 'Y' and two nails knocked through the tops of the arms of it. The bomb aimer would look through the peep hole and when the two nails coincided with the towers on the dam he would press the release. It was simplicity itself and, when tested, proved to be superbly accurate.

On 28th March, air to air radio tests took place, the first time this had been tried in bombers (later to be used a great deal in conjunction with the 'Master Bomber' technique). On this occasion a range of 40 miles was achieved. On 7th April, with two aircraft flying between 500 and 15,000 feet, a range of only 30 miles was achieved. In one of the aircraft flew Guy Gibson and Wg. Cdr. Wally Dunn, the tremendously experienced Chief Signal Officer of 5 Group. The test was hopeless with continental 'mush' making communications impossible.

On 11th April, Gibson flew down to Manston in a Miles Magistar, taking with him F/Lt. Bob Hay, an Australian who was to fly with F/Lt. Mick Martin as his bomb aimer and also as the squadron bombing leader. Back at Scampton S/L 'Dinghy' Young was left 'looking after the shop'. They went down to witness the trial bomb dropping at Reculver in Kent, a few miles west of Margate. At Reculver there were two stone towers, remains of a church which had been constructed from the remains of the Roman fort of Regulbium which had formerly stood on the site. The twin towers on the otherwise fairly featureless and barren stretch of coast were chosen as the release point for the bombs. Unfortunately the trials were unsuccessful, the bomb broke up on impact with the water.

The return journey back to Scampton was also eventful when the engine of the Magistar failed while over Margate at a height of about 300 feet. Somehow Gibson managed to make a crash landing, hitting a tree in doing so; they were unhurt although the aircraft was a write-off. When a doctor drove up to help and found them unhurt he said, 'It's a shame they make you fellows fly so young.'

They needed for the training a full moon period, but over the period left there were only a few nights with suitable moon conditions. Necessity is the mother of invention and a system known as 'Two Stage Blue Day Night Flying', was invented by two brothers, both squadron leaders, Arthur and Charles Wood. The system gave night conditions in the cockpit for the pilot, navigator and bomb aimer by the use of amber glass goggles, with the cockpit perspex covered with a blue filter component. Gibson had five aircraft fitted out with this on the 15th and another four at the end of the month. He went along to Waddington, where this work was being undertaken, climbed into the Lancaster and sat in the pilot's seat and tried on one or two pairs of goggles, looking at the instrument panel in front of him to see what effect they had. He seemed satisfied by what he saw and two further aircraft were modified.

By now Wallis knew the drop height would have to come down to 60 feet from 150 feet and on 24th April trials began at a speed of 210 mph at the new height. On 28th April, a bomb was dropped from 60 feet at a speed of 258 mph, it bounced four to five times and carried on for a distance between 600 & 700 yards. On 5th May, Gibson got his operational aircraft ED932-G and made a flight, testing the spotlights at 60 feet.

The bombs to be used on further trials and those that were to be used on the actual operation began to arrive; 37 were delivered to Scampton and 19 to Manston for further tests. Since the beginning of training 31 exercises had been flown and 168 drops made, of which 52 had been successful. On 2nd May Gibson wrote a letter to the Senior Air Staff Officer (S.A.S.O.) at No 5 Group HQ, saying that P/O Watson, the armaments officer, had just arrived back from Manston after a 3 week attachment during the trials with 'Upkeep'. After he had interviewed him he was astonished to hear that during his three weeks at Manston he had been shown files, diagrams and a map of the objective and other secret information concerning 'Upkeep'. He had, apparently, been shown these files by W/C Gardner who was in charge of the trials at Manston. Gardner had, in Gibson's opinion, done a fine job organising the trials but Gibson ended by saying that he felt the more people knew the details of 'Upkeep' the less secret it would become.

On 4th May, Wally Dunn, the communications officer, said that he felt VHF (Very High Frequency) was the only answer to the communication problem. A test that day using the previous methods had, once again, proved hopeless. The only solution, it seemed, was the TR 1143 transmitter as used in fighters and which had never been used in bombers before. By the evening of 9th May, 18 Lancasters had been fitted with the fighter-type radios. A further test on 11th May was held and on this occasion good communication was maintained up to about 50 miles.

Gibson was, in the meantime, at Manston testing a modified aircraft with 'Upkeep' and reported a drop at 60 feet and a good run of 600 yards. Trials were carried out on the ground, spinning the bomb at 500rpm, which looked like the front wheel of a steam roller, and took some 30 to 40 minutes to stop spinning once the motor had been stopped.

On the 13th, further sorties was carried out by the PRU from Benson to cover the Eder and Sorpe Dams. This was to ensure that the Germans had not got wind of the attack and brought in further defences. On the 14th, a sortie from Benson was made on the Möhne Dam but failed to cover the dam itself but careful checking of the relationship between the edge of the water and the sides of the valley showed that it had risen in February and was, by then, probably only about 6 feet below the top of the Dam.

Also on 14th May, a full dress rehearsal was carried out at Uppingnam over the Colchester Reservoirs at 22.00 hrs, about the time they would get airborne on the night of the Op. In Gibson's aircraft flew Group Captains Whitworth, Maudsley, and P/O Shannon. On the 15th, a final photograph sortie was made. This was successfully carried out and a report was drafted by F/O d'Arcy Smith during the night of the 15/16th and issued early on the morning of the 16th. Having seen the report the AOC of No 5 Group, Ralph Cochrane, gave the word that the operation was to take place the next night.

CHAPTER SEVEN

THE DAMS RAID

The code name for the three primary dams had come from Air Commodore Bufton, Director of Bombing Operations, on 10th May: Möhne Dam - *Objective X*, Eder Dam - *Objective Y* and Sorpe Dam - *Objective Z*. Other codes words for the operation were: *Goner* - the code name for the bomb, *Nigger* - meant the Möhne had been destroyed, *Dinghy* - meant the Eder had gone, and *Zebra* - the Sorpe. *Codfish* was the code name for the reserve crews to be called up and their code word to attack target X was *Pranger*. The call sign used by all crews was *WB1*.

On 15th May, all the pilots and navigators were told the target, but were instructed not to tell the other members of the crew. They would not be told until 10.00 hrs on the 16th, at the longest briefing in the history of Bomber Command held in the airmen's huge dining room. At the door were posted three guards, 'No one in or out', was the order of the day until the briefing was over. The code words and wireless transmission procedure were detailed and of the original 21 crews, 19 were selected. P/O Divall, who had arrived late for training, and F/Lt Wilson who had some form of illness in his crew were left out.[1]

In trials four aircraft had been damaged; four days before the actual operation two had to go away for repair and just two days before the operation two more aircraft were damaged on a cross country flight and were in need of repair. Having worked minor miracles the last aircraft returned from repair at 21.07 hrs on the evening of the 16th, only minutes before take off. The briefing was attended by the Station Commander, weather-, signals- and station officers, along with the AOC 5 Group, Ralph Cochrane, and Dr Barnes Wallis. The AOC stood up first and said,

---

[1] - See Appendix 2 for the detailed list of crews.

'Bomber Command has been delivering the bludgeon blow on Hitler, you have been selected to give the rapier thrust which will shorten the war, if it is successful.' It was then Gibson's turn. He had the honour, or otherwise, of pulling back the curtain to show the target for that night - the moment they had all been waiting for, or dreading. There were large photographs of the dams, and the scale models made at Medmenham. He outlined the flight plan, departing Scampton in three waves, attacking the Möhne, Eder, and Sorpe in that order.

21 - PRU photo of the Möhne Dam just prior to the raid. Note the torpedo nets on booms.

THE DAMS RAID

MÖHNE DAM - GUNNE near SOEST (GERMANY)
G.S.GS 4416. Sheet Q 2. Lat. 51 29' N.
RB 226214. Long. 08° 04' E.

| 0 | 500 | 1000 | 1500 | 2000 | 2500 | 3000 FEET |

Plan dated 1913   (1 6,000)   approx.   Issued January 1945

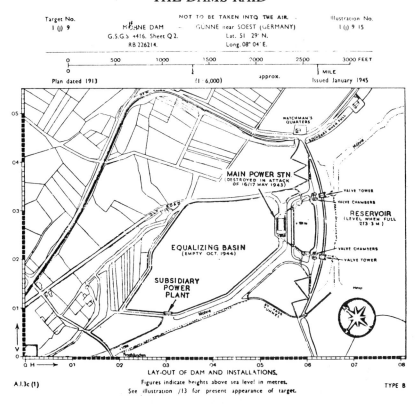

LAY-OUT OF DAM AND INSTALLATIONS.
Figures indicate heights above sea level in metres.
See illustration /13 for present appearance of target.

A.I.3c (1)   TYPE B

Target map of the Möhne Dam

The first wave of five aircraft would be led by S/L McCarthy and take the northern route, but would cross the enemy coast at the same time as the leading three aircraft of the second wave. This consisted of nine aircraft, in three sections, spaced at ten minute intervals, and led by Gibson in the leading three; they would take the southern route. McCarthy's group would attack Sorpe acting as a diversion for the Gibson's group who were attacking the primary targets, the Möhne and Eder. The third wave of five aircraft would be held in reserve on route until called upon, depending on the success of the first two waves. They would also fly the southern route and their take off time would coincide, hopefully, with the confirmation that the first

103

two waves had successfully breached all three dams and that they could return to base (see route map on page 115).

In British airspace the flying altitude was set at 1500 feet QNH[2], but on crossing the English coast they would descend to just 60 feet using the spotlights to determine their height from the sea. The deputy leader to Gibson was Young, and if he fell out Maudsley was to take over as deputy. In the cramped cockpits the crews worked as a well-practised team with the pilot flying the aircraft and maintaining course, the navigator checking position and watching the altitude like a hawk, the bomb-aimer checking the distance to run to the target and constantly running through the procedures for the dropping of the bomb, and the flight engineer checking his panel and the speed.

The attack on the Sorpe was to be different in that the aim was to drop the bomb by flying the length of the Dam from end to end and to aim at hitting the water near the centre of the dam wall, about 20 feet out. This was to be as low as possible and at a speed of 180 mph, slower than the attack on the other two dams. Between each attack, three minutes was allowed which made sure the water had subsided and the extent of the attack could be judged.

For the attacks on the Möhne and Eder each wireless operator was to fire a red Very cartridge to let the leader know he had attacked and released the bomb. Each aircraft was to fly a left handed circuit in the target area to avoid collisions and to give the pilots the clearest view of the target area. At the briefing no less than 41 sets of instructions had to be read and learned by the crews.

[2] - *QNH - 'Q' Code for altimeter sub-scale setting for MSL (mean sea level). As distinct from QFE which is for the altitude above runway threshold.*

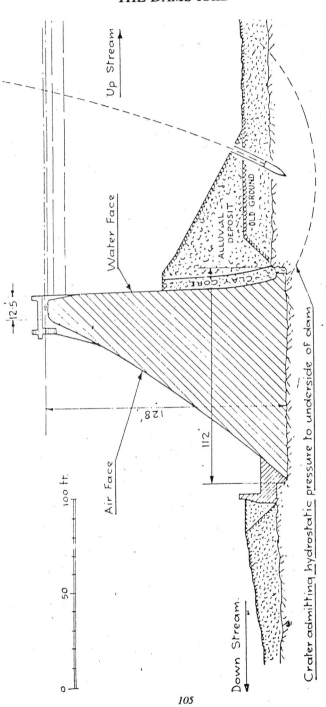

CROSS SECTION OF MÖHNE DAM — RUHR VALLEY

The main briefing over Gibson then handed over to Wallis who said 'I feel very humble and honoured, tonight you are going out to show what this weapon will do.' He went on to explain more about the dams and their importance. Outside at the dispersals the bombs were being loaded in the aircraft, still warm to the touch from being filled with the four tons of high explosive. The final reconnaissance flight had shown torpedo nets in front of the Möhne dam in a double boom, and 3-inch anti-aircraft guns on the banks to the north of the dam, while on the dam itself there were possibly three to four light guns in the towers. The total weight of each Lancaster at take off was 63,000 lbs, which included 1750 gallons of petrol.

22 - Gibson's Lancaster 'G' George stands ready with bomb attached.

Bombed and fuelled up the Lancasters stood ready to go and the crews, now fully briefed, waited to don their flying kit ready for take off. The only blight and very personal sadness for Gibson, as well as the Squadron as a whole, was that Gibson's dog, Nigger, had been run over outside the main gate and killed. His body was taken into one of the cells in the guard room, the idea being that Gibson was not told until after the operation.

However, quite by accident, he was told and, of course, was very upset - the dog had been his friend and constant companion for two years. He asked 'Chiefy' Powell to bury the dog outside his office in No 2 Hangar at midnight, the time he would be over the target.

23 - Nigger's grave at Scampton as it is today.

The 16th was a fine warm day and one of great activity at Scampton, 1500 men and women would be involved in getting the aircraft off that night. The Adjutant had a problem in getting the traditional operational meal of eggs and bacon for the crews because, to keep the maximum security, 617 were not down as flying that night. It was only by a nod and a wink to the catering NCO that things were smoothed over and the crews got their meal. The crews were all doing last minute things like writing letters. Gibson was checking and re-checking, making sure all was well. John Pulford, Gibson's flight engineer had compassionate leave to attend his father's funeral in Hull and was escorted there and back by RAF Police. There were some onlookers who, no doubt, thought he was a deserter and under escort back to prison!

The crews were out at their aircraft for about 20.30 hrs, David Shannon was a little late getting on the transport from the officers' mess, probably saying goodbye to his girlfriend, Ann, who was a WAAF officer. Gibson was very relaxed and looking fit as he stood chatting to the ground crews despite the upset of losing Nigger earlier in the day. Finally came the order to load up, the pilot first, followed by the flight engineer, navigator, wireless operator, bomb aimer, and the two gunners at the back. The air was full of the whining of starter motors as they turned the Merlin engines over one by one, spluttering into life and clearing before settling down to a steady rumble. Inside the aircraft the flight engineers watched as the oil pressures and coolant temperatures rose, ready for take off. The pilots ran through their 'after starting' checks with the crew: 'External power supply removed and clear; radiator shutters open; booster coil off; vacuum pumps changeover cock, suction reading; flaps operational check, up, selector neutral; check on all fuel tanks with booster pumps on and off; engine temperatures and pressures within limits...' Then would come the pre-taxi checks, pre take-off checks and finally the clearance to set the brakes and ease the throttles to full boost.

The Sorpe wave were down to take off first but the leader, F/Lt McCarthy, had problems with his aircraft and did not get off until 22.01 hrs, using a spare aircraft. The other three got off with Barlow first at 2128 hrs followed by Munro, Byers and Rice. It's strange to record that McCarthy, although away last and on his own, was the only one of this wave to reach the target and drop his bomb. Gibson and his wave were next to go; all three Lancasters with Gibson, Hopgood, and Martin took off together at 21.39 hrs. The next three, Young, Maltby and Shannon went off at 21.47 hrs. The remaining three, Maudsley, Astell and Knight took off at 21.59 hrs.

For Wallis it was a case of just waiting at HQ No 5 Group; he had asked to fly with Gibson, and wanted to see it through to the end but this was sympathetically turned down. It was not long,

22.57 hrs in fact, before the first problems arose. An aircraft was seen to be hit by anti-aircraft fire over the Dutch coast and crash near Texel. Sgt Byers and his crew were killed outright, an experienced crew with six weeks intensive training and they only reached the Dutch Coast - it didn't bode well.

Geoff Rice was also in trouble as he reached the Dutch Coast, he probably realised, after seeing Byers go down, that he must fly lower, but this of course had its dangers. As he flew down the Zuyder Zee (now Ijsselmeer) with the moon reflecting off the mirror-flat sea it became increasingly difficult to accurately judge the altitude of the aircraft. Eventually he flew too low and the bomb was torn away from the belly of the aircraft as if a hand had come out of the water and pulled it off. As it was wrenched aft it tore through the bodywork of the aircraft, finally hitting the tail wheel which was forced up into the aircraft, breaking the main spa of the tailplane and finishing up in the Elsan closet near the rear door. Although the bomber was only in contact with the sea for a few moments it shipped a huge volume of water through its gutted belly and the rear gunner, F/Sgt Burns, was nearly drowned as what was probably a couple of tons of water surged aft through the fuselage. Further forward, all the little inspection panels in the floor of the flight deck and above the bomb bay were spouting water, saturating McFarlane's charts. After heaving the Lancaster clear of the water Rice took stock, there was nothing for it but to return to base. The next stage was to run the gauntlet of searchlights and flak on the island of Vleiland, and fly back to Scampton, a journey of three hours twenty minutes. At Scampton he had to make a landing on his main wheels only and hold the tail up as long as possible. As he slowed down and finally came to halt the tail fins hit the runway with a terrible crash.

After getting out Geoff sat on the grass and began to feel his world had come to an end, all that training for nothing and above all he felt he'd let the squadron down. As he ruminated a car pulled up with Charles Whitworth, the station commander, in it. He took the crew back to the ops room where no less than 'Bomber' Harris was waiting for them. After he had been told the story of how they lost their bomb he just said, 'You are a very lucky young man.' Geoff had been expecting the dressing down of a lifetime, but Harris's sympathetic attitude was far more appropriate and was to have a lasting effect on Geoff.

In the meantime Gibson and his group had reached the Dutch Coast and, around Haltern, Gibson came under fire from light flak and all three leading aircraft were picked up by searchlights. Adopting standard evasive action he put his aircraft into a steep dive and turn before continuing on his way across Holland. Hopgood's aircraft had been hit in the engagement and damaged with three of the crew, including Hopgood, wounded.

At this time, back at Scampton, George Powell with the help of Cpl John Bryden, had the sad job of burying Nigger in front of No 2 Hangar and in view of Gibson's office. The grave was marked with a simple wooden cross.[3]

Les Munro was flying en route to the Sorpe Dam and, with McCarthy still trying to catch up, he was leader. At 22.57 hrs they were crossing the Zuyder Zee when they came under accurate fire from a flakship and was hit amidship, the inter-com and radio were put out of action which meant they could not communicate in the air as was planned. It was decided between them that they had no alternative but to return and they landed at Scampton at 00.36 hrs. Before that, at 00.11 hrs, Gibson had come under fire, and in the same action Astell hit a low tension wire and crashed on the Dutch/German border.

Gibson reached the Möhne dam at 00.15 hrs and began his bomb run at 00.25 hrs. As soon as he came in sight of the towers they came under intense flak fire which his gunner,

---

[3] - *The grave is still there today and is tended and looked after by a civilian, although 617 Squadron have long since left. The wooden cross has long since been replaced with the beautifully inscribed stone.*

George Deering, returned as best he could. At 00.28 hrs P/O Spafford pressed the release and the bomb fell away, bounced three times and slammed right into the dam. Gibson logged his speed at the time at 230 mph and his rear gunner reported a huge gush of water from the dam but when it subsided the dam was still intact.

David Shannon described the dam as looking like the model but larger than they had expected. He saw Gibson's bomb explode and throw a column of water 100 feet into the air.

At 5 Group HQ Harris, Cochrane and Wallis waited for news, the first signal that Wally Dunn picked up was the flak warning from Gibson, and then that he had dropped his bomb, but no apparent breach.

24 - Wally Dunn, Chief Signals Officer No. 5 Group (taken in 1945).

When the water had subsided Gibson called in 'Hoppy' Hopgood and it was his already damaged aircraft that Karl Schutte, a flak gunner on the dam, saw approaching with its spotlights gleaming on the water. It would appear that the bomb was dropped too late and instead of hitting the dam wall it bounced over and blew up the dam power house on the other side. Hopgood's aircraft had been hit in the attack by the flak put up by Karl and his gun crew and was on fire. It crashed soon afterwards but not before two of the crew had managed to bale out to be taken prisoner.

It was then the turn of Mick Martin and Gibson called him up to give him the 'Go' and at the same time told him he would fly across the length of the dam to draw some of the flak from

Martin. Despite this Martin's aircraft was hit a number of times on the run in and was lucky that his starboard outer fuel tank

25 - Karl Schutte's flak gun crew on the morning after the raid.

was empty when it was hit. His attack was successful, but when the waters subsided the dam still stubbornly held. The next aircraft came in flown by Young and again was successful but there were still no signs of a breach. Gibson was certain, however, that one more bomb would do it, and so sent Maltby in. Adjusting speed and height Maltby aligned the heavy Lancaster between the twin towers of the dam and watched the tracer snake towards him and felt the shells bursting around the aircraft as they sped towards the release point. The aircraft lurched upward as he heard 'Bomb Gone!' on the intercom and they flashed over the dam. The bomb bounced four times before hitting the dam wall, sunk to the trigger depth of the hydrostatic pistols and then exploded. This time, as the huge column of white water settled, it was clear that the dam had been breached and millions of gallons of water were pouring from it. At this time Gibson was flying around, but could not see the explosion owing to smoke in the air and spray on his windscreen. He was about to order David Shannon in when he saw the breach in the dam and the water pouring through, changing his instruction and ordering Shannon to hold off. When he took a closer look the breach was about 150 yards long. Back at No 5 Group the signal *'Nigger'* broke to great jubilation.

Gibson circled for a few minutes and then called Maltby, and Martin, sending them back to base. At Scampton the reserve force had taken off, Ottley first, followed by Burpee, Brown, Townsend, and finally Anderson.

By this time Joe McCarthy had in fact reached the Sorpe Dam and made a run at 00.46 hrs, but it wasn't right and he went round again and again, finally dropping his bomb on the tenth run. He reported a column of spray rising to an estimated 1,000 feet the resulting damage was a crumbling on the dam wall of about 15 to 20 feet. His speed at the time of the attack was logged at 180 mph compared with that at the Möhne Dam of 230 mph. It was 03.00 hrs before McCarthy reported back that he had dropped his bomb, by which time he was only 23 minutes away from landing at Scampton. He arrived back with a bullet hole through the undercarriage which had burst the starboard tyre. How he got this is unknown as there were no defences at the Sorpe Dam.

In the meantime Gibson, along with Young, who although now without his bomb was to act as deputy leader if needed, Shannon, Knight, and Maudsley made for the Eder Dam through the valleys while keeping a sharp eye on the mountainous ranges which towered above their route. It took about 10 to 15 minutes to reach the Eder from the Möhne. David Shannon made a dummy run on a bridge which he then realised was not the dam and so circled around waiting for Gibson to positively identify the Eder. He then told Shannon to make his approach, there were no torpedo nets, and no flak because the Germans apparently thought the terrain itself offered adequate protection. After five unsatisfactory runs Shannon was told to fly a holding pattern and Maudsley was called in. It appeared that his aircraft had been damaged en-route and when he dropped his bomb it left the aircraft late and hit the parapet on the top and exploded. One weak call on the R/T was heard from him, but nothing else. About 30 minutes later, and on fire, his aircraft was engaged by anti-aircraft guns and crashed, and all the crew were killed.

By this time both Astell and Burpee had been shot down and crashed. It was the turn of Shannon once again and at 01.39 hrs and at a speed of 220 mph, he dropped his bomb, it bounced twice and hit the dam wall and exploded, making a breach of about 9 to 12 feet in the wall from which water was seen to be pouring out. In next was Les Knight, the quiet, unassuming Australian, who had been recommended for the DFC after a fine tour with 50 Sqdn, but somehow did not get it. He was told by Gibson on the radio that he had the last bomb and to make it a good one. On the first run P/O Johnson, the bomb aimer, was not happy and so around they went again escorted by the ever faithful Gibson. The next run was a good one, the bomb bounced three times, hit the dam and exploded, creating a much larger breach with and a water spout 800 feet high. The water was now crashing down the valleys taking everything with it, houses, bridges, nothing could withstand this tidal wave some 30 feet high. At 01.54 hrs Gibson told 'Hutch' to make the signal 'Dinghy' signifying the Eder had gone as well.

At 02.10 hrs Group signalled to Gibson, asking him how many aircraft of the first wave were available, he replied 'None'. On the return trip Young was shot down near the Dutch coast and he and all his crew were lost. Shannon had flown back to the Möhne and saw the valley filling up with water, and then hedge hopped home, about 50 miles from the Möhne his gunners shot up a train which had stopped. He said later 'I quite enjoyed our six week's training for the attack, but during that time we knew nothing about the target.' Shannon arrived back at Scampton at 04.06 hrs, followed by Gibson at 04.15 hrs and Les Knight at 04.20 hrs.

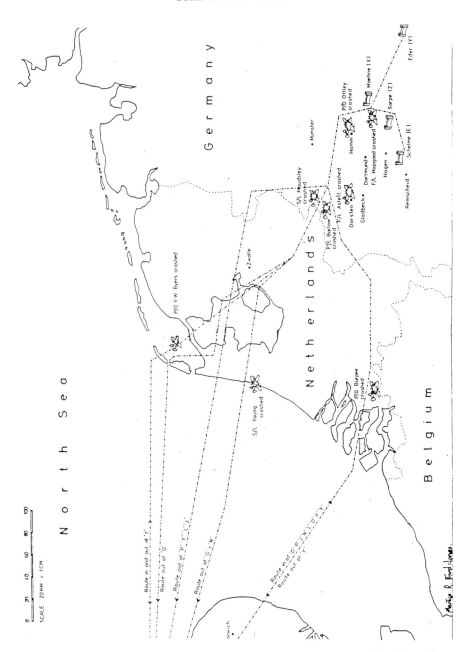

Route map in and out for the crews of 617 Squadron (Martyn Ford-Jones).

The reserve group, of which only Brown, Townsend, and Anderson were left, had been given instructions to attack, Brown and Anderson were to attack the Sorpe, and Townsend the Ennerpe. Ken Brown attacked at 03.14 hrs but it took ten runs before he was satisfied enough to drop his bomb, once again it hit the dam wall and crumbling of about 300 feet was seen. Cyril Anderson was unable to find the dam because of mist in the valley and he was coned by searchlights but unable to knock them out because his gunners had stoppages, he came back with his bomb intact and landed at 05.30 hrs.

Bill Townsend made three dummy runs on the Ennerpe Dam before dropping his bomb at 03.37 hrs. After the second bounce the bomb made contact with the wall and exploded but no damage was observed. He returned in broad daylight over Texel, and Holland and observed en-route that the flood waters had reached the Emms Canal. He was the last to land at 06.15 hrs.

When Martin landed he was met by Wallis who, when he saw the gaping hole in the wing where the shell had gone through the petrol tank, said 'Oh my God!' As another damaged Lanc landed the 'flesh and blood' involvement came over to him. As a scientist he had been totally involved in the development of the bomb and the tactics of the raid and had not, until then, thought of possible casualties. When he learned of the losses he said, close to tears, 'Micky, if I had known I would not have started it.' He was a very simple, humble man and in his opinion his greatest achievement was four children and 20 grandchildren.

When Gibson arrived back at his office he threw the brass detonation key which armed the bomb to 'Chiefy' Powell and, to this day, it is still in his family and has been proudly mounted on a wooden plaque. On the morning of the 17th, Peggy Paterson was parked outside the officers' mess and saw the crews return and begin a party to celebrate the operation and, in the circumstances, simply being alive. They came out of the mess and poured beer all over the engine of her car.

| YEAR 1943 | | AIRCRAFT | | PILOT, OR | 2ND PILOT, PUPIL | DUTY |
MONTH	DATE	Type	No.	1ST PILOT	OR PASSENGER	(INCLUDING RESULTS AND REMARKS)
						TOTALS BROUGHT FORWARD
MAY	7	LANCASTER	V	SELF	USUAL CREW	TO MANSTON - A.A.E.F.
MAY	8	OXFORD	U	JRCF	S/L SMITH	TO HENDON.
"	"	VEGA ?	7	6RCF	F/L COX	HENDON - MANSTON.
"	"	OXFORD	U	S/L SMITH	JRCF	MANSTON - BASE.
"	11	LANCASTER	P.	JRCF	USUAL CREW	LOW LEVEL. OPREEP. DROPPED AT 60 FT.
"	14	"		P.	JRCF	PROG ROW OF 6 TODAYS BOMBING LOW LEVEL
"	14	"		P.	" "	AND V.H.F. TEST.
				P/O WHITWORTH. D.S.O. D.F.C		FULL DRESS REHEARSAL ON DERWENT LAKE AND COLCHESTER RES. CONNECTED SUCCESSFUL
"	16	LANCASTER	G	SELF	SGT PULFORD P/O DEERING P/LT TAERUM ??? P/LT HUTCHISON P/O SPAFFORD P/O TREVOR.	LED ATTACK ON MÖHNE AND EDER DAMS. SUCCESSFUL.

GRAND TOTAL [Cols. (1) to (10)]
1924 Hrs. 20 Mins.

TOTALS CARRIED FORWARD

Gibson's Log Book entry for the Dams Raid - simple and to the point

117

BORN LEADER

In Gibson's log book a simple entry for 16/17th May, 'Led attack on the Möhne and Eder Dams - Successful.' Time recorded for the operation was six hours forty minutes.

Reference :-
DO/5/43.

No. 617 Squadron, R.F. Station,
Scampton, Lincs.

20th. May, 19 3.

My Dear Mrs Gillespie,

It is with deep regret that I write to confirm my telegram advising you that your son, Pilot Officer R. Gillespie, is missing as a result of operations on the night of 16/17th. May, 1943.

Your son was Air Bomber of an aircraft detailed to carry out an attack against the Mohne Dam. Contact with this aircraft was lost after it took off, and nothing further was heard from it.

It is possible that the crew were able to abandon the aircraft and land safely in enemy territory, in which case news will reach you from the International Red Cross Committee within the next six weeks.

Please accept my sincere sympathy during this anxious period of waiting.

I have arranged for your son's personal effects to be taken care of by the Committee of Adjustment Officer at this Station, and these will be forwarded to you through normal channels in ... .

You will notice that I have addressed your son as Pilot Officer Gillespie. This is due to the fact that information was received yesterday that he has been appointed to commissioned rank. Had he been with us, I am sure he would have received the heartiest congratulations on this well deserved award, from all ranks of the Squadron.

If there is any way in which I can help you, please let me know.

Yours Very Sincerely,

P. Gibson

Wing Commander,
Commanding, 617 Squadron, R.F.

Mrs. R. Gillespie,
111, Currook Rd.,
Carlisle.

One of the sad letters which Jim Heveron was tasked to type in the days which followed the raid.

THE DAMS RAID

No. 617 Squadron,
R.A.F., Station, Scampton,
Lincoln.

7th July 1943.

My dear Mrs Astell,

Many thanks for your letter which I received
to-day, and thanks very much for your congratulations.

I know how terrible this suspense must be, but
please believe me when I tell you that there is absolutely
no news yet. There is also no news of the safety of any
of the other crews.

Bill's aircraft was not actually seen to blow
up for certain, although an aircraft in the distance was
seen to go down, and subsequently blow up. This aircraft
may have been one of four of the missing ones, so it is
impossible to say which. There is no danger of the flooding
endangering the lives of the airmen who baled out.

With regard to your last paragraph, whether there
is a possible chance of Bill having escaped, I am afraid
I can't possibly tell you as Bill's formation leader did
not return, and I myself never saw him throughout the
whole journey.

Once again, please accept my deepest sympathy
in your great anxiety.

Yours Very Sincerely,

G. Gibson

Mrs. M. Astell,
    Spire Hollins,
        Chapel-en-le-Frith,
            Derby.

*A letter of consolation written later by Gibson confirming
that there was still no news of the missing crew.*

BORN LEADER

Inside the officers' and sergeants' mess there were 56 empty chairs for breakfast; only twelve hours before they had been filled with happy but apprehensive young men with a sense of adventure, now those same young men were no more. Gibson dictated letters for the next of kin and added a personal message to each one.

_____

DAMBUSTERS - MARCH

Words from the 46th Psalm

God is our strength and refuge,
Our present help in trouble;
And we therefore will not fear,
Though the earth should change
Though mountains shake and tremble,
Though swirling waters are raging,
God the Lord of Hosts is with us evermore

There is a flowing river,
Within God's holy city;
God is in the midst of her,
She shall not be moved
God's help is swiftly given,
Thrones vanish at His presence;
God the Lord of Hosts is with us evermore

Come, see the works of our Maker,
Learn of His deeds all powerful;
Wars will cease across the world
When he shatters the spear
Be still and know your creator,
Uplift Him in the nations;
God the Lord of Hosts is with us evermore

CHAPTER EIGHT

THE RESULTS

On the morning of 17th May, a reconnaissance was made of the area of the dams and photographs taken. The bulk water from the Möhne Dam had gone 16 miles down the valley, and from the Eder, 20 miles. At the Sorpe, which had not in fact been breached, water was seen seeping out into the basin below. A further reconnaissances on the 18th showed a minor breach in the Ennerpe, damage caused by Bill Townsend's bomb.

26 - Conversations I would like to have overheard. German policemen observe the damage caused by the flood waters from the Möhne Dam.

27 - *The wreckage-strewn basin of the Möhne Dam on the morning of 17th May. Note the barrage balloons brought hastily into service.*

28 - *A slightly different view of the basin showing the bedrock exposed by the scouring waters of the flood.*

*29 - A PRU photgraph of Kassel showing some of the
flooding from the Eder Dam.*

On the 16th, before the raid, the Möhne had an estimated 132 million cubic feet of water behind it, on the 18th it was only 14.4 million. A German report, dated 24th June 1943, said the breach was 76 metres wide and 21 - 23 metres deep and it was estimated that it would take 2,000 men to repair the breach. A further report on 20th December 1944, stated that Gibson's bomb had exploded in front of the torpedo netting and tore the net barrage near the left sluice gate of the dam, it also stated that John Hopgood's bomb had in fact destroyed the power plant for the dam, cutting off the electricity for the whole valley. It is important to note that the report went on to say that not all the bombs fell in the same area but were ideally spaced and that the last bomb, the fourth, exploded in the centre of the dam. The examination afterwards confirmed that the cracks were confined to the area between the two sluice towers.

A special questionnaire was formatted in which each crew was asked a set ten questions about the raid. Gibson was asked at what range he saw the target (Möhne). His reply was, three to four miles. How many bounces did the bomb make? He replied three. How many runs did he make? The reply was just the one. He commented that VHF communications were perfect, a tribute to Wally Dunn and his team. In the case of Mick Martin the range which he saw the target was one a mile and a quarter, owing to the smoke and spray from Hopgood's attack. He also commented that the formation commander had done a great job by diverting the gun fire from the target towards himself, and that his whole crew had done their job well. Dave Shannon reported seeing the Eder from three miles, and that he had shot up a train at Cösfeld. Big Joe McCarthy said he saw the Sorpe from 5 miles away and that he had seen the dam crumbling for a distance of about 15 to 20 feet. After Ken Brown's attack he said he saw crumbling for about 300 feet, his flight engineer, Basil Feneron, said he saw two large breaches at the Möhne Dam and water pouring through both. They also confirmed they had made ten runs on the Sorpe before releasing the bomb. Bill Townsend went via the Möhne Dam to the Ennerpe and saw the roofs of houses sticking up above the water.

In Germany the rescue work went on non-stop for about 90

hours, and it was eight days before the SS troops, who had been specially drafted in, went back to their barracks. Albert Speer, the German Armaments Minister, arrived the day after the raid and surveyed the damage. He immediately summoned experts from all over Germany, had the electrical installations dried out, and obtained replacement pump motors from other factories to be installed so that the Ruhr industries would be supplied with water in the shortest possible time. He also sent a personal report to Hitler, and several thousand men were transferred from the Atlantic Wall to start repairing the dams. The German drawings of the repair required showed the breach in the Möhne to be 60 metres wide and 17 metres deep. The area of the repair on the Eder was 60 metres wide by 24 metres deep. Speer also inspected the Sorpe Dam, which had in fact held, the breach being slightly higher than the water level.

The result of the attack was that two of Europe's largest dams, containing more than 300 million tons of water, were practically drained and widespread damage was done by flooding. The raid deprived the Nazis of power and the loss of a water supply was of far-reaching importance requiring supplies to the industrial consumers to be dramatically reduced. General supplies of water to the *Rhurgebiet* (the whole Rhur area) had to be curtailed for some time. The great mystery is why the dams were not attacked while under repair, the scaffolding was wooden and would have easily been destroyed. It would only have been a matter of keeping the breaches open up to the rainy season and the effect of sustained loss of water for the Ruhr industries would have been grave. It was one of the things that Wallis had originally advocated in his own plan, keeping the dams breached so they did not build up in the winter rains.

The Germans themselves began to experiment with a bouncing bomb, their's being called *'Kurt'* and which was rocket assisted but had the same two hydrostatic pistols and one time fuse. At the end of the war some 850 were found in store, nearly complete, at Marienfeld. The first experiments had come directly

30 - Headline in the Daily Telegraph on the morning of the 18th May.

after the attack on the Ruhr Dams in May, 1943. Dr Lambrich was asked to develop an *Überwasserbombe* (overwater bomb). In a dossier compiled by the Germans they said 617 had been known after the raid as 'The Dam Raiders', 'The Dambusters' and 'Gibson's Boys'. They got their information on the dams raid from cuttings from The Times, Daily Telegraph and the New Chronicle, all of 18th May, 1943. Another report came from the Manchester Guardian of 20th May, 1943.

CHAPTER NINE

THE DAMS CELEBRATIONS

On 18th May 1943, messages of congratulation were coming from all walks of life. Lord Trenchard sent a message to Harris, as did Portal, and Harris was summoned to Buckingham Palace for His Majesty to give him his personal congratulations. In turn Harris sent a telegram to Barnes Wallis congratulating him on the success of his weapon. Sir Stafford Cripps also sent a message to Wallis and to all members of the Ministry of Aircraft Production on behalf of the War Cabinet and the Secretary of State for Air. In his reply Wallis described the men of 617 as 'Incomparable Young Men'. General Eaker, commanding the US Eighth Air Force, sent Harris a message which said:

> 'Will you accept the congratulations of the American Air Forces and express to the gallant crews which executed this magnificent task, our admiration for this great work.'

The Daily Telegraph, which in those days cost one penny - ha'penny had, as its front page on the 18th:

'RAF Blow Up Three Key Dams in Germany'

Another headline on the front page was:

'Pilot Sees Breach in Dam by Moonlight'

'Success at Fourth Attempt'

(This was the story of Guy Gibson's efforts of course). Another said:

'He Drew the Enemy's Fire'

At this time Gibson was running around on an ancient two-stroke motorcycle on which, it would appear, he was not very proficient because he seemed to fall off quite a lot. He was a hazard for the MT Drivers who were worried about running him over. Around about this time Peggy Paterson (nee O'Neill) was asked by Gibson if she would like to serve on an operational squadron, she replied she would. Shortly afterwards she was posted to Scampton and became his driver. 'I really enjoyed being W/C Gibson's driver and I missed him when he left, he was always a gentleman.'

On 19th May, Gibson was recommended for the Victoria Cross by Air Chief Marshal Sir Arthur Harris. The recommendation showed he had flown 242 hours on Hampdens, 199 Hours on fighters, and 200 hours on Lancasters. A full two page account of the Dams raid formed part of the recommendation and it was submitted to the King on the 22nd May for his approval by the Secretary of State Sir Archibald Sinclair. In Gibson's log was a typically modest note which simple read: 'Awarded VC 23.5.43.'

He had been troubled with a carbuncle before the raid and went into the RAF Hospital at Rauceby for a few days while it was treated. While there a WAAF nurse, Mrs Backhurst, who worked in the operating theatre was asked by Gibson if she would take his tunic to the hospital tailor to have the ribbon of the Victoria Cross sewn on. The tailor was delighted to have such an honour and said he would return the tunic in person.

Of the men who carried out the raid, 34 were recommended for awards and all were approved, this included 5 DSOs, 4 Bars to the DFC, 10 DFCs, 2 CGMs and a Bar to the DFM (the only one awarded to 617 Squadron during the war) and 11 new DFMs.

RECOMMENDATION FOR IMMEDIATE AWARD.

Christian Names ...GUY PENROSE........... Surname GIBSON, DSO & Bar, DFC & Bar.

Rank .Squadron.leader.(Acting.Wing... Official No ..39438...........
           Commander)

Command or Group 5.Group.Bomber.Command Unit ..617.Squadron,...........

Total hours flown on operations :
                           1st Tour (Hampdens)   242.30
                           2nd Tour (Fighters)NIGHT 199.45
                           3rd Tour (Lancasters)   200.44

Recognition for which recommended .....Victoria.Cross,.............

Appointment held ....Officer Commanding, No. 617 (B) Squadron.

PARTICULARS OF MERITORIOUS SERVICE.

On joining Bomber Command in the early days of the War, this then junior Officer quickly established a reputation as an outstanding operational pilot.   Not content with taking the fullest possible share in all normal operations, he developed a habit of going out alone during his "rest" nights to make single-handed attacks on, for instance, such highly defended objectives as the German battle-ship "Tirpitz", then completing in Wilhelmshaven.   At the conclusion of **his** first operational tour on night bombers, he persistently demanded to remain on operations.   He was, therefore, transferred to night fighters for his "rest" period, in preference to a training unit.   At that time the foundations of the night fighter organization were being laid, and this by then highly experienced night pilot took a leading part in raising and indoctrinating new night fighter formations.   During this period as a night fighter pilot, although stationed in a part of the country comparatively free from raids, and with night fighting tactics and equipment in the elementary stage, he destroyed at least three enemy bombers over this country.   At the conclusion of this tour as a night fighter pilot, he again insistently demanded to be returned to night bomber operations.   As a Squadron Commander his second operational tour on bombers was marked by consistently outstanding achievements, both as an operational pilot and as the leader of his squadron.   On the conclusion of this his third operational tour, he again raised the most strenuous protests against relegation to non-operational duties. He was therefore given command of a unit then forming for special tasks.   It was as the Commander of this unit that he led the attacks on the Moehne and Eder Dams.

It is typical of this Officer that he himself made the first attack on the Moehne Dam, thus taking the full brunt of the anti-aircraft defences while still at their best.   After delivering his attack with great accuracy from a height of a few feet, he proceeded to supervise the remainder of the attack on the Moehne Dam.   In the process he deliberately and repeatedly circled round at a very low altitude directly over the anti-aircraft defences for 30 minutes in order to attract their fire to his own aircraft and to enable his gunners to shoot up the gun positions, thus leaving the remaining aircraft, which were attacking the Dam in turn, as free as a run as possible.   After the Moehne Dam had been breached he withdrew the remainder of his force and led them to the Eder Dam.   Having already expended his own projectiles, he pursued similar tactics while the attack on the Eder Dam was successfully developed. Throughout both attacks he maintained a minute by minute commentary thus enabling reserve forces to be accurately disposed.

The recommendation for the Victoria Cross (see overleaf)

BORN LEADER

This young Officer is beyond doubt the most inspiring leader, efficient operational captain, and outstanding fighting airman of the Command. Of a quiet and unassuming manner, and possessing an unfathomable store of personal courage, he displays all greatest qualities of leadership including intelligence and organizing ability of the highest order. He is as insatiable in seeking the post of greatest danger as he is imperturbable in the encounter.

For extraordinary courage, exceptional leadership and example in the face of the enemy over three and a half years of hazardous operations culminating in the successful attacks on the Moehne and Eder Dams, which he personally led and wherein he displayed, as is usual with him, the highest valour in the face of deliberately sought and tremendous additional risk, this Officer is most strongly recommended for the award of the Victoria Cross.

Air Chief Marshal,
Commanding-in-Chief,
BOMBER COMMAND.

19th May, 1943.

On 27th May, the King and Queen visited RAF Scampton, where the whole raid was explained to them and photographs shown of the damage to the dams. The King and Queen were shown an aircraft with the bomb loaded, and Barnes Wallis showed them how it worked. An account of the visit and a photograph of the King, with Gibson, was on the front page of the Daily Telegraph on the 28th. Among others present were Charles Whitworth and Ralph Cochrane.

The designs for a Coat of Arms was submitted to the King for his approval by Gibson, one showed a hammer parting the chains on the wrists of Europe, with the motto - 'All the Map'. The second, which Gibson liked best, showed a breached dam in the centre with the motto - *'Apres moi Le Deluge'* (After me the flood). It was left to the Chester Herald experts to give their opinion and to decide.

31 - The King viewing photographs of the dams, 27th May 1943. Ken Brown behind the King, Lance Howard behind Gibson and Joe McCarthy to Gibson's right (Imperial War Museum).

32 - The King chats to 'Mick' Martin with Whitworth in the background and Gibson to his left (Imperial War Museum).

33 - The Officers' Mess at Scampton 22/5/43 (l to r) Anderson, Townsend, Howard (r), Hutchison (f), McCarthy (r), Rice (f), Martin, Wilson, Munro, Gibson, Fort (r), Shannon, Hobday, Buckley, Maltby, Johnson, Knight, Taerum, Spafford, Chambers, Trevor-Roper.

CONFIDENTIAL

HEADQUARTERS

EIGHTH AIR FORCE

ETOUSA

OFFICE OF THE COMMANDING GENERAL

May 18, 1943.

Air Chief Marshal Sir Arthur T. Harris, KCB.,OBE.,AFC.,
A. O. Commanding-in-Chief,
R.A.F. Bomber Command,
High Wycombe,
BUCKS.

Dear Air Chief Marshal Harris,

I have just listened to a grand presentation by
Squadron Leader Robinson of your raid against the German dams.
For more than a year now I have had the privilege and the pleasure
of observing the legerdemain and black magic of the Old Master !
As you know, I count that a great privilege and a rare opportunity.
I must say, however, that I think even you exceeded your own very
high standard in conceiving and executing this last daring plan.
It appears now that it was easily the outstanding bombing effort of
the war.   To have accomplished that with 19 Lancasters is a
remarkable tribute, not only to keen target selection, but it
represents a rare refinement in the appreciation of the force
required to accomplish a task.

Will you accept the congratulations of the American
Air Forces and express to the gallant crews which executed this
magnificent task, our admiration for this great work.

Sincerely,

IRA C. EAKER
Major General, U. S. A.
Commanding.

*Letter to Sir Arthur Harris from Major General Ira Eaker
of the American Eighth Air Force.*

Gibson was now in great demand as a national hero, towns
launching savings drives asked for him to visit and if he could go
he would. He said, 'I'm not tactful. I tell them the truth. I tell

them whatever the papers say there is nothing in this war a civilian can do which will equal the sacrifice asked of those bomber crews who go out to Germany night after night, losing about 30 bombers each time until their turn comes and goes, or just comes. I tell them there's nothing they can do to equal that, but they can try by giving money.' At Maidstone, a small Kentish town, they asked for £750,000. Gibson was the main attraction and they paid £1,750,000.

He also said, 'A man's not normal if he's not frightened. Even after dozens of raids there's a tightening of the stomach as you approach the target and you realise in the next ten minutes you'll be alive or dead. It's like going into a cauldron. The sky and the earth cease to be normal. The searchlights form the ring of your cauldron. The incendiaries are the bubbling brew; the flak and the spent flak smoke are the sparks and steam. Only when you're actually in the cauldron does the fear depart entirely and your training takes charge of you. It's the difference between waiting in the wings to go on and then doing a well rehearsed act. If you drop your bombs accurately there's a terrific feeling of elation. You feel like the plane, lighter and more buoyant.'

Gibson took Eve to Cornwall for a while, taking the leave that had been postponed and had, by then, been so well earned. They went out fishing in a 30 foot smack with an old sea-faring man, Dick Perkin. Starting at 5am they cast their lines and marked them with a float. At noon they would return to haul in their catch; one day they pulled in a large skate, a huge monk fish, and a 12 foot shark. Other days were spent just walking with Eve along the cliffs, and looking for gulls' eggs which they had for supper.

Even as he climbed aboard his aircraft on the night of the raid he had thought of Eve. As he turned at the door of the aircraft and a Air Ministry photographer took a photograph he shouted 'Make sure you send a copy to my wife!' The rest of the crew roared with laughter, and said 'Send a picture to his wife, as though he wasn't coming back.' Maybe he thought he might not make it and at least she would have the last photograph taken of him.

Gibson smoked cigars as well as cigarettes and a squat little well-charred pipe. Cigar smoking amongst aircrew was rare, they were usually confined to the older intelligence officers, the MO, or the Adjutant, but Gibson liked a cigar and used to say to hell with the cracks that were made about it.

In early June awards were announced to the groundcrew staff. Charles Whitworth, endorsed by Gibson, recommended awards for F/Lt Caple, P/O Watson, W/O Taylor, Sgt Chambers, F/Sgt's Smith, Gover, and Campbell, who were all engineers, armourer's fitters or instrument makers. Added to this was W/C Wally Dunn, the Chief Signals Officer at 5 Group; W/C Brown, the Group Engineering Officer; S/L Goodwin, Group Armaments Officer. Also, Gp Capt Satterly and Gp Capt Whitworth himself were awarded Commendations for Meritorious Service.

On 28th May a message was sent to Sir Arthur Harris from the American General Bradley. In it he said:

> 'I cannot refrain from again expressing my admiration for the splendid job of dam busting which you so ably pushed through to successful conclusion.'

On 21st June the men who were to be decorated on the 22nd set off from Scampton and left Lincoln Station at 2.20 pm. They had a specially reserved part of the train for the 45 who made the journey. On the 22nd the time for arrival at Buckingham Palace was 10.15 am and each man being decorated was given tickets for two relations or friends. It came as a surprise to all when instead of the King taking the investiture it was to be Her Majesty Queen Elizabeth, The King was away at the time in the Middle East. It is normal for the VC to be awarded at the end of the ceremony but on this occasion Guy Gibson was the first to

INVESTITURE

AT

BUCKINGHAM PALACE

on *Tuesday, the 22nd June, 1943,*
at 11 o'clock a.m.

THE VICTORIA CROSS.

To be Decorated :—

Wing Commander Guy **Gibson**, Bomber Command (also to receive a Bar to the Insignia of a Companion of the Distinguished Service Order).

Under Wing Commander Gibson's inspiring leadership, his Squadron has executed one of the most devastating attacks of the war—the breaching of the Moehne and Eder dams. The task was fraught with danger and difficulty, and he personally made the initial attack on the Moehne dam. Descending to within a few feet of the water and taking the full brunt of the anti-aircraft defences, he delivered his attack with great accuracy. Afterwards he circled very low for 30 minutes, drawing the enemy fire on himself in order to leave as free a run as possible to the following aircraft, which were attacking the dam in turn. He then led the remainder of his force to the Eder dam where, with complete disregard for his own safety, he repeated his tactics, and once more drew on himself the enemy fire so that the attack could be successfully developed.

THE DISTINGUISHED SERVICE ORDER.

To be Companions :—

Squadron Leader David **Maltby**, Bomber Command,

Flight Lieutenant Harold **Martin**, Bomber Command,

Flight Lieutenant Joseph **McCarthy**, Royal Canadian Air Force, Bomber Command (also to receive the Decoration of the Distinguished Flying Cross),

Flight Lieutenant David **Shannon**, Royal Australian Air Force, Bomber Command,

Pilot Officer Leslie **Knight**, Royal Australian Air Force, Bomber Command.

THE DISTINGUISHED FLYING CROSS.

To receive a Bar :—

Flight Lieutenant Robert **Hay**, Royal Australian Air Force, Bomber Command,

Flight Lieutenant Robert **Hutchison**, Bomber Command,

Flight Lieutenant Jack **Leggo**, Royal Australian Air Force, Bomber Command,

Flying Officer Daniel **Walker**, Royal Canadian Air Force, Bomber Command.

To be Decorated :—

Flight Lieutenant Richard **Trevor-Roper**, Bomber Command,

Flying Officer Jack **Buckley**, Bomber Command,

Flying Officer Leonard **Chambers**, Royal New Zealand Air Force, Bomber Command,

Flying Officer Harold **Hobday**, Bomber Command,

Flying Officer Edward **Johnson**, Bomber Command,

Pilot Officer George **Deering**, Royal Canadian Air Force, Bomber Command,

Pilot Officer John **Fort**, Bomber Command,

Pilot Officer Cecil **Howard**, Royal Australian Air Force, Bomber Command,

Pilot Officer Frederick **Spafford**, Royal Australian Air Force, Bomber Command

Pilot Officer Harlo **Taerum**, Royal Canadian Air Force, Bomber Command.

THE CONSPICUOUS GALLANTRY MEDAL.

To be Decorated :—

Pilot Officer Kenneth **Brown**, Royal Canadian Air Force, Bomber Command,

Pilot Officer ~~Flight Sergeant~~ William **Townsend**, Bomber Command (also to receive the award of the Distinguished Flying Medal).

be decorated and along with his VC he received the bar to his DSO, awarded at the end of his tour with 106 Squadron[1]. The Queen asked him if he had all his fellow 'raiders' with him and he said he had, although in fact they were one short as John Pulford, his engineer, was sick and had to wait until November for his DFM.

34 - Roy Chadwick, designer of the Lancaster bomber, with Gibson at Buckingham Palace.

Roy Chadwick was also decorated with the CBE for his work and designing of the Lancaster bomber without which they would have lacked the means to deliver the bombs. Many photographs were taken outside the Palace and the Queen, hatless and wearing a spray of roses, had a word for each man who was decorated. What a special occasion it was for the men from Australia and Canada, although it is sad to record that many

[1] - *This made him the most highly decorated airman of WW II*

35 - Buckingham Palace June 1943 (l to r) Sumpter, Taerum, Buckley, Spafford, Trevor-Roper, Maltby, Johnson, Martin, Heal, Gibson, Hobday, Shannon, Franklin, McCarthy, Oancia, Fort, Wilkinson, Chambers, Webb, Chalmers.

never made it back to their homeland to tell their families. It was the first time an investiture had been held by the Queen of England since Queen Victoria.

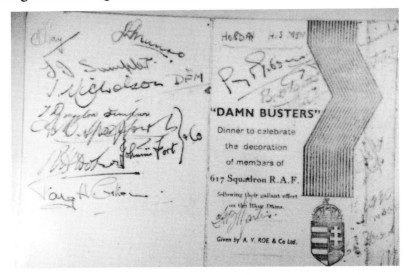

36 - A rather faded copy of the menu for the celebration dinner on which was printed "DAMN BUSTERS".

Guy Gibson left the Palace by a side entrance, few people seeing him go. But later, in his West End Hotel, he was caught and interviewed by the Daily Mirror. That evening a celebration dinner was hosted by A V Roe[2] in the Hungarian Rooms, Dorland House, Lower Regent Street. The menu carried the words 'Damn Busters' in error, but the corrected form of Dam Busters soon caught on and has stuck to this day. The music was provided by Jack Hylton and his band and during the evening Gibson signed a large photograph of the breached Möhne Dam, his signature being right in the breach. The remainder signed on the right-hand side of the breach. It was then presented to Barnes

[2] - Founder of the AVRO aircraft company

Wallis, and now resides in the RAF Museum at Hendon. Gibson was presented with a model Lancaster, in silver, by the A V Roe Company (AVRO). Gibson's comment was:

> 'The success of the attack on the dams was due to hundreds of technicians and above all to the Air Officer Commanding the Group and the Senior Staff Officer. We flying crews are indebted to them all.'

CHAPTER TEN

POST DAMS

In June 1943, Gibson paid a visit to Maidstone, near West Malling, his old fighter airfield. While there he visited the local Scout troop the 1st Tovil (Maidstone, Kent) Troop. He had been in the Scouts way back in his school days in Folkestone and was very proud of his membership; on his left wrist he wore a stout leather band with the insignia of the Boy Scouts. The motto of the Scouts is *'Be Prepared'* which was very apt when going out night after night to face flak and night fighters.

37 - Gibson, third from the left, reconfirming his scout promise at Maidstone.

While with the Maidstone Troop he reaffirmed his promise as a Scout in the Headquarters of the Troop where the Scoutmaster, Mr Glad Bincham, was an old friend. Also present, making their promise as Tenderfoots, were Group Captain E Colbeck-Welch DFC, Wing Commander Richards AFC, Flt Lt Davidson, all from the RAF, and, from the Army, Lt Carruthers of the Royal Artillery. Each made the following promise:

> *'On my honour I promise to do my best,*
> *To do my duty to God and the King,*
> *To help other people at all times,*
> *To Obey the Scout Law.'*

Gibson then addressed the Scouts saying:

'It is a great honour and a great privilege to reaffirm my promise to my King and country here with you in your 1st Tovil Troop. I was a Scout a long time ago. I am afraid the only thing I passed was my cooking test, but it did teach me in the time that I was a Scout the decent things in life. The Nazis, they have the German Youth Movement, where they are taught the foulest things in life. You are quite the opposite; you are taught resourcefulness, courage, and devotion to duty - in other words, you are just being taught the things which will stand you in good stead in the service, and so I say to you: Good Luck, and best wishes for the future!'

The Scouts were stood in a half circle and Gibson shook hands with every member of the troop, newsreel cameras were present at the time.

Also in June 1943 the Hollywood Director Howard Hawkes had just completed a film 'Air Force', which was about the US Flying Fortress operations, and was planning a United Nations film about the Chief Allied Nations to depict the fighting spirit of each nation and wanted the Dams story for his contribution on the British fighting spirit. He was willing to contribute a considerable amount of money to the Benevolent Fund in return and wanted Gibson to speak for about two and half minutes about the raid. This was left on ice for a while.

On 20th July 1943, Gibson and Eve were invited to spend the weekend at Chequers as guests of the Prime Minister and Mrs Churchill. On the 21st, he and Eve were picked up by car from the Ritz Hotel where they had spent the night and taken to Chequers.

On 2nd August 1943, he made one trip with 617 Squadron in the crew of the new commanding officer S/L George Holden, the target a Flying Bomb site at de Cassan in France.

In August 1943, Gibson was invited by the Prime Minister to make a goodwill tour of the USA and Canada, officially it was called a Ministry of Information Lecture tour. He left London on the 4th for the Clyde where he boarded the Queen Mary with Churchill, his wife and daughter Mary, who was in the ATS, and any many other famous names: General Wavell, who had flown from India; Brigadier Wingate, who had led the 14th Army in Burma; the three Chiefs of Staff; Lord Mountbatten, the Chief of Combined Operations and 200 others from Britain. The ship sailed on the 5th at 5.30 pm and landed in Halifax, Nova Scotia on the 9th. The journey to Quebec was made by train. Churchill was going on for the Quebec Conference known as 'Quadrant'.

On 20th August, Gibson flew in a Lockheed aircraft from Quebec to Montreal, and then on to Oshawa. On board was Air Vice Marshal Billy Bishop VC, of WWI fame. Gibson is recorded in his log book as having flown the aircraft in a journey of two hours and thirty minutes. On the 21st, he flew from Oshawa to Toronto, although the pilot on this occasion was P/O Young. And so the tour went; 22nd, Toronto to Jarvis and back to Toronto; 23rd, Toronto to New York; 24th, New York to Toronto. On the 26th, in a Hudson aircraft, Toronto to Winnipeg; 29th, in a Crane aircraft, Winnipeg to Yorkton; and using the same aircraft, on the 31st, Yorkton to Moose Jaw. 1st September, Moose Jaw - Dafo; 6th on to Mossbank, and on the 8th to Calgary. There he met the mother of Harlo Taerum, his navigator on the Dams raid. She said how proud she was to meet him. Gibson said how pleased he was to meet her and that her son was the living image of her. He went to her home in Calgary and spent several hours with her. Only eight days later Harlo, flying with George Holden, was to be shot down and killed.

38 - Gibson at Calgary. In the background is Mrs Taerum mother of Harlo Taerum, his navigator on the Dams Raid. She was also to lose another son, Lorner, an air gunner, killed on 3rd February, 1945.

He was given a general salute and welcomed by Air Vice Marshal Howsam MC, commanding No 4 Training Command, he mentioned the crews under training would be dam-busting,

Cologne-busting, Hamburg-busting and finally busting Hitler's phoney fortress of Europe. At Calgary he also met 'Dinghy' Young's brother, Robert, 'Dinghy' of course having been lost on the Dams raid. Robert was training to be an air gunner and Gibson told him, 'Pilots aren't everything, other members of the crew have just as important a part to play.'

On the 12th, he flew on in a Goose aircraft to Vancouver and Victoria. On the trip of the 14th, to Montreal, he mentioned in his log book how nice one of the air hostesses was.

The tour and talks went on to the 24th, taking in a number of towns and cities in Canada. On this stage of his journey he flew in an Avro Anson and when he arrived at Oshawa, on the 24th, he stayed in the Selgnory Club to recover. From here on his tour was in the USA and he flew in various aircraft and took in Kansas, Pittsburg and Orlando. On 12th October, he flew to Washington from Miami, a seven hour journey, to be invested with the Legion of Merit (Commander), by General 'Hap' Arnold, of the US Air Force.

On 27th October, he visited Hollywood and met Howard Hawkes and on 12th November, he returned to New York. Finally, on 1st December, he returned to Prestwick from Montreal. On his return the question of a film being made by Howard Hawkes was raised again. Gibson spoke to Air Marshal Peck about it and his view was that the Air Staff would warmly approve the film being made. A letter to this effect was sent to Mr J Beddington, Director of Films Division at the Ministry of Information, by the Public Relations Department at the Air Ministry. It would appear that nothing came of this as no film was ever made.

When he visited his old school, St Edwards, he was asked by the boys to speak about his flying and he said 'Well, when I was a boy here Old Boys used come down and say they never did any work. Don't believe them. I worked like hell!' That and a smile is all they got.

One of Gibson's hobbies was photography and he brought

back three reels of cine-film from his tour of USA and Canada where he made about 150 speeches and broadcasts. On his return Gibson was posted on 3rd January 1944, to the air Ministry Directorate - Prevention of Accidents, as Deputy Director. It was about this time that he wrote his book 'Enemy Coast Ahead' which he had, apparently, been ordered to write. To help him with this, Jim Heveron[1] was given a 48-hour pass which, being a Londoner, suited him fine. Gibson wanted Jim to bring details from the 540/541 Operation Record Book. Jim found Gibson in a small back room at the Air Ministry, then in the Kingsway. He had let his hair grow long and he seemed very depressed; he was almost in tears when he saw Jim and he said, 'The bastards won't let me fly, except for a bloody desk, I'm a bloody prisoner in a cage!' He opened the window and all one could see was a brick wall of the building opposite. Jim left the material he wanted with him and asked Gibson if he would give him a reference so he could get a job at the end of the war. This he promised to do and a few days later it arrived on Jim's desk. It was a top-class reference and helped him to secure a good job in 1946.

On 9th February 1944, Gibson was on the short list to become Conservative Candidate for Macclesfield, in place of a Mr Garfield Weston, the Canadian millionaire biscuit manufacturer, who was retiring. He had been short-listed from the original list of twenty seven. He paid a visit to the Division and appeared at meetings with Lord Vansittart at Macclesfield and Congleton. He said that if he were elected his post-war planning would be health, housing, and employment for the boys coming out of the services. The other four candidates were also in the services, but some years older than Gibson who was then 25. Mr Weston MP said, 'I think he is a great fellow, and has the making of a great

---

[1] - *Who had been one of the senior NCOs allocated to 617 Squadron when it was formed at Scampton.*

man.' He was leaving politics to go into industry but Gibson later decided his heart wasn't in politics and turned down the invitation[2]. At the same time he visited the AVRO works and spoke to the thousands of workers who were making the Lancaster bomber. He is reported to have taken his wife, Mr Weston and, his secretary, Mr Butler, for a flight in a Lancaster but there is nothing in his log book recording the flight.

Left to right: Mr. Roy Chadwick, C.B.E., Director and Chief Designer of A. V. Roe & Co. Ltd.; Wing Comdr Gibson; Mrs. Gibson; Mr. Weston; and Mr. R. H. Dobson, C.B.E., Managing Director of A. V. Roe & Co. Ltd.
[By courtesy A. V. Roe & Co. Ltd]

V.C. Sees Lancasters Built

WING Commander Guy P. Gibson, V.C., D.S.O., and Bar, D.F.C. and Bar, rounded off his visit to Macclesfield by touring an Aircraft factory in Manchester district and a local silk mill last Thursday.

AIRMAN DIES IN FLYING ACCIDENT

2 - The man who got the position in 1945 was another airman - Air Commodore Arthur Harvey - Now Lord Harvey of Westbury.

While at the Air Ministry he was invited to the BBC and Roy Plumley's programme *Desert Island Discs*. His first choice was *The Warsaw Concerto*, followed by *Where and When* - this was connected with his wife, Eve, and how he met her in 1940. He also chose *The Flying Dutchman* because of his love for the sea, the march *From the Shores of Tripoli* and a Bing Crosby record, which reminded him of the Bing Crosby imitations he had heard over the inter-com when flying. He also chose the *RAF March* which he confessed still gave him a shiver down his spine whenever it was played. The Strauss Waltz *Thousand and One Nights* and, finally, *The Ride of the Valkyrie* ended his eight tunes.

On 13th March, he went on Staff Officers' War Office Course No 12 at RAF Uxbridge, then to No 28 Group, where he remained until 12th June 1944, when he was posted to No 55 Base at East Kirkby to become Base Operations Planner. Here he managed to fly one operation with S/L Millichap and his crew in Lancaster LM 216-N of 630 Squadron on 19th July, 1944; the target was Thiverny nr Creil, 25 miles NW of Paris, a Flying Bomb site and supply dump. From his log book he appears to have flown as first pilot, a superb bombing photograph was brought back by Gibson, who bombed from 18,000 feet.

On 2nd August, he moved up the road to No 54 Base at Coningsby. While there he managed to get a lot of non-operational flying in but on 18th August, in a Lightning (LOB 26) with a S/L Ciano, he made a flight to Deelen Airfield and recorded it as his 74th bombing op. His next operational flight was with W/C Woodroffe in a Mosquito letter D to Le Havre, flying time three hours five minutes. Up to 19th September 1944, he had only nine hours and thirty-five minutes flying in on the Mosquito.

CHAPTER ELEVEN

THE LAST MISSION

The last flight recorded in Gibson's log book was on 16th September 1944, in a Lightning aircraft from Langford Lodge to Coningsby, a flight of one hour and five minutes. In September 1944, he had been given permission by Cochrane to fly on operations again, provided he took a Mosquito Pathfinding course at Warboys. This was essential if he was to take on a marking role as Leonard Cheshire had done with 617 Sqdn earlier in the year. In the opinion of Group Captain Hamish Mahaddie, the recruiting officer for the Pathfinders, a short course at Warboys, and then on to the PFF[1] 'Mossie' Unit would have benefitted him greatly. Sadly he did not go on the course, and if Cochrane had known he had not been checked out at Warboys he would have withdrawn permission for him to fly on 19th September, 1944.

The operation on the 19th was to Munchen Gladbach and Rheydt. The target had two important railway lines, one from Aachen and the other from Cologne, which met at Rheydt before running on to Munchen Gladbach some two miles away, then connecting with the main route from the Ruhr to Venlo and Holland. Large railway yards, capable of handling 2,500 waggons every twenty four hours, and several important engineering works were also there, together with factories making railway signalling apparatus, cables, electric generators, motors, transformers, and oil tank installations. The targets were of great importance and were consequently strongly defended by flak and fighters.

A force of 236 Lancasters and 10 Mosquitos were despatched for the operation, one Mosquito flown by Gibson as the Master

[1] - *Pathfinder Force*

*39 - Ten days before Gibson's last fatal flight he enjoys
a drink with other officers at the Petwood Hotel - 617's Mess.*

Bomber. The time over the target was 21.45 hrs to 21.57 hrs. The main force of the bombers was picked up and plotted by German radar at 21.10 hrs 50 miles SW of Liege, and again at 100 miles from the target and once more at 21.30 hrs on the last leg to the target. However for some unknown reason those plots were not passed down the German chain of command until 21.43 hrs when the bombers were actually approaching the target.

Gibson was due to use a Mosquito based at Coningsby but this became unserviceable and he went over to 627 Sqdn at Woodhall Spa. The CO, W/C Curry, authorised KB 267-E[2] for him to use.

[2] - *Normally flown by F/O 'Johnny' Johnson with navigator F/O Brian Harris.*

*40 - Gibson talks with Sir Archibald Sinclair, Secretary of State
for Air, at Conningsby (Imperial War Museum).*

41 - S/L Jim Warwick who was to navigate for Gibson.

He had in fact taken up the unserviceable aircraft in the morning for its NFT (Night Flying Test). His navigator was to have been P/O Dai Thomas, who at the last minute went down with the flu, an illness which was to save his life. His place was taken by a S/L Jim Warwick who was, like Gibson, based at Coningsby. Warwick had arrived at Coningsby on 25th August 1944, having completed a tour with 49 Sqdn on 14th January. He had been awarded the DFC and in his recommendation for the award was the fact that he had completed 25 operations and also mentioned that he had taken part in the raid on Peenemunde in August 1944. Much of his tour of operations had been through the Battle of the Ruhr in 1943. Jim had been born in Belfast on 10th October 1921 and had worked as a civil servant at the Air Ministry in 1939 up to the time he was called up on 1st September 1941.

Sergeant Neve[3] recorded taking off with 101 Sqdn at 19.12 hrs and finding 10/10 cloud over the target area. Over Rheydt F/Lt Kennedy DFC reported a very large explosion which lit up the whole sky for a second or two. W/C Ron Churcher, who was responsible for the marking of the target, spoke to Gibson by radio over the target. The weather he reported was bad with low cloud which made it difficult to see the results of the attack. The marking was reported to have been accurate and was followed by

[3] - *Later Squadron Leader*

a concentrated attack on the first aiming point, but at the second aiming point it was thought the Target Indicators had hung up in Gibson's aircraft.

John Hereford of 101 Sqdn said, 'Gibson came on the air to say that he could not see the target and was dropping below cloud level.' After some time had gone by and he did not come back on the air, the Deputy Master Bomber took over for the rest of the raid. The official reports state that the aiming point was eventually marked and the bombing appeared good. Gibson was heard to say on the air 'Okay, that's fine, now home' - the last contact recorded with Gibson and Warwick.

42 - *The site of the crash on the van der Riet farm. The actual point of impact was still discernable in 1989 but since then building has covered the site.*

Some three-quarters of an hour later he was seen with what appeared to be flames coming from his aircraft over Steenbergen in Holland and crashed in a field of a farm run by Mr van der Riet. He remembers the Germans sealing off the area within half an hour of the crash. The Deputy Mayor of Steenbergen reported:

> *'At 23.30 hrs on the Territory of the
> Municipality in the West Graff Henrik Polder,
> about one and half miles from the centre of the
> municipality, a British aircraft 'Merlin KB 267
> Lockheed 22 Mark 33 crashed in flames.'*

Near the crash an identity plate or disc was found with the
following written on it: *J.B. Warwick Offr Press 156612
RAFVR*; and a sock with the name 'Gibson' on it. The machine
had circled sometime over the municipality and was totally
destroyed on impact, supposedly by the explosion which threw
the crew out. Identification of the bodies was apparently
impossible because they were completely torn apart and terribly
mutilated. The remains were carefully gathered and put in one
closed coffin, and buried in a special grave in the manor usual
in that municipality in the local Roman Catholic cemetery. The
burial was done at the expense of the town and in the presence
of the Pastor of the Reformed Church and the Roman Catholic
Priest. Attached to the coffin were metal plates with the names
of the victims and the date of the crash. Found at the scene of
the crash were the following:

One silver ring, gold plated with the initials J.B.W
ID plate with J.B. Warwick Offr Press 156612 RAFVR
A damaged wristwatch mark 'Omega'
Two clasps
One black tie
A booklet with the title: Instructions and hints for fishing and
general information.
An envelope with address:
S/Ldr J.B. Warwick D.F.C , Officer Sen, RAF Station,
Coningsby, Lincoln.
A list with the heading: Travelling Aircraft Servicing Form.

THE LAST MISSION

One sleeve button.
A piece of uniform.
One sock with 'Gibson' marked on it.
A forage cap.
A small portfolio with stamps.
5 maps.
A cartoon cover.
20 banknotes of 100 French Francs*.
6 banknotes 100 Belgium Francs*.
2 banknotes 50 Belgium Francs*.
2 banknotes of 25 Guilders*.

* all from the escape kit.

All these items were deposited in the town hall and were sent to the Information Centre of the Netherlands Red Cross at Zwarteweg. Tuesday, 19th September 1944, is known as *Dolle Dinsdag* which, translated, means 'Mad Tuesday', not that many people saw what happened to Gibson because curfew was at 20.00 hrs. The people of Steenbergen wanted a ceremonial funeral but the German Commander ordered the burial within the hour. The man who buried Guy Gibson and Jim Warwick, Mr Sloven, still lives in Steenbergen.

The other casualties from this raid were light, only 4 Lancasters; F/O Leonard of 619; F/O Findlay 467; and F/O Brindley and F/Lt Fee from Gibson's old squadron 106; and one Mosquito, W/C Gibson of 54 Base. Two were shot down by fighters over the target at 21.45 hrs and 21.53 hrs, a third near Turnhout, and a fourth over the Dutch Islands.

When Sgt Neve arrived back at base he found out that Guy Gibson was missing. The Intelligence Officer in the debriefing said his aircraft had gone down in flames, adding that it was possible that, because he was so low over the target and because of the bad cloud, someone had bombed early and hit him, but this of course was only speculation. It would appear that bombs had been dropped a fraction too early and before he could clear the area.

43 - Winter 1944. The original grave and single marker at Steenbergen.

S/L Rupert Oakley, the former CO of 627, theorised that the most significant factor in Gibson's failure to return was that he had not enough operational hours in on the Mosquito. Gibson had at most eleven hours on Mosquitos and Jim Warwick had none. The changing over of petrol cocks so as not to starve the engines of fuel at a critical time can give the impression the aircraft is on fire because white flames come from the exhaust pipes if one is slow in changing from a empty tank to a full one. Another point was that on the Mosquito, when flying low, if you pushed forward on the stick to hug the contours of the land the engine would cut out with the negative 'G' and then, after a second or so, would recover. At night this recovery was accompanied by quite a flare from the exhausts. Again this maybe what the eye witness in Steenbergen saw. If Gibson had been close to stall and pushed forward on the stick to gain speed it would have been fatal at low altitude.

R, CONGLETON COURIER, AND STOCKPORT E

FRIDAY, DECEMBER 1, 1944.   **134th**

WING COMMANDER GIBSON, V.C. MISSING

W/CMDR. GUY P. GIBSON AND MRS. GIBSON.

WING COMMANDER GUY P. GIBSON, V.C., D.S.O. and Bar, D.F.C. and Bar, who might have become M.P. for Macclesfield had he not withdrawn his nomination, is missing.

He failed to return from an attack on Reydt, near Munchen-Gladbach, on the night of Sept. 19th when, as a master bomber, his job was to fly much lower than the main force of aircraft to direct the operati ns.

He was heard over the target giving unhurried in-structions, and finished his job. He was not heard again.

W Cdr. Gibson first visited Macclesfield in February as a guest of Mr. W. Garfie d Weston, M.P., at the dinner which the Member gave at the Maccles-field Arms Hotel in honour of Lord and Lad y Vansittart.

HEARTY WELCOME

Lord Vansittart addressed a meeting of A.R.P. personnel at the Whiston Street Head-quarters about the "Win the Peace" movement, of which he is President, and Wing Comdr. Gibson, who supported him on the platform, was given a rous-ing reception. During his stay in Macclesfield the Wing Com-mander visited Adlington Hall and Maternity Home, toured the premises of Messrs. Edmund Lomas, Ltd., silk manufacturers, Waters Green, Macclesfie'd, and those of Messrs. A. V. Roe and Co., where the Lancasters he led on the Dams raid, and so gained his V.C., were built. He was accompanied on these visits by Mrs. Gibson.

Recommended by the Ad-visory Committee of Maccles-

Local Home Guards

To Attend Royal Review

TWO Macclesfield members of the Home Guard who are to attend the special parade in Hyde Park, London, on Sunday to signalise the "stand down" of the force, will be the only holders of their ranks from the whole of Cheshire to take part.

They are Lieut. E. Kirby, of "A" Company, 9th Battalion, and Company Sergeant Major J H. Broadhurst, of "A" Coy., 8th Battalion. Lieut. Kirby's home address is 61 Knowsley Road, and C.S.M. Broadhurst lives at 8 Fowler Street.

In all, six representatives of the two local battalions will be present at the review by the King, the other members of the party being: Ptes. F. Morton ("E" Coy), 3 Nicholson Ave.; G. Minshull ("C"), 99 Canal Street, Congleton (8th Battn); Ptes. G. White ("B"), 6 Flash Lane, Bollington, and W. H. Sherratt ("A"), 35 High Street (9th Battn).

The men are described as having been selected as com-pletely representative types of Home Guards.

(Continued from previous col.)

field Conservative and Unionist Association in March for adop tion as prospective National Conservative candidate for the Division, he announced in Sep-tember his reluctant decision to forgo his selection for Parlia-mentary duties in order to de-vote the whole of his time to his Service career.

He had taken part in al-most 200 operations, being in the first attack of the war— on the Kiel Canal.

His wife, formerly Miss Evelyn Moore, of Penarth (Glam), used to be an actress. W Cmdr. Gibson met her while she was appearing at Coventry.

Another unanswered part of the puzzle is that a distance of 81 nautical miles from the target to Steenbergen took 45 minutes to fly, when it should have been 20 at the most.

When Gibson failed to return that night and was posted missing a security clamp was put into operation. At that time they didn't know he had crashed, only that he was missing. For all they knew he might have baled out and be evading capture. If that was the case they didn't want the Germans to be on the alert to pick him up, with his reputation after the Dams raid it is not difficult to imagine that the Germans would have been delighted to have Gibson as their 'guest'. No one outside the operations room at Coningsby or Woodhall Spa knew, except Rupert Oakley. However, at about 7am, only a matter of hours after his being posted missing, a navigator from 627 hitched a lift to Lincoln in a long distance lorry. He was amazed to hear the driver say to him, 'That was tough luck on Guy Gibson last night' Another navigator of 627, Andy Denholm, said, 'I remember the day he went missing. On that day in the Flight Authorization Book he named the target prior to departure which was against regulations. My understanding was he only went to view the raid and was not officially participating.'

It was only when Steenbergen was liberated that correct identification was made and two wooden crosses put up to their memory. Later, after the war, the Commonwealth War Graves put up two of their magnificent headstones which are what can be seen today. It's interesting to note that officially Gibson and Warwick were recorded as being with 627 Sqdn at the time of their death, when in fact, although using a 627 aircraft, they were both at 54 Base, Coningsby.

Eve Gibson was sent a personal letter from Winston Churchill, expressing his sadness at the news of her husband's death. A move was made to recommend him for a posthumous bar to his VC, but that came to nothing. To sum up the evidence surrounding his failing to return the most significant factors must relate to his lack of operational flying over a period of 18 months following the Dams raid, not enough flying hours on the Mosquito, and failing to take the Pathfinder course at Warboys. It was a sad end to such a formerly outstanding career as an officer and as an airman.

CHAPTER TWELVE

POST WAR

In December 1946, McGowan Cradon offered his services as 617 Squadron's historian. He was an intelligence officer and had been recommended by Group Captain Leonard Cheshire VC, a former CO of 617 Squadron. Cheshire himself had been asked to take on the task of writing the history of 617 Squadron, and had consented, but then his other work forced him to drop any idea. However, Cradon's offer was rejected as it seemed he had spent more time than his masters cared with the aircrew of 617, and got in many practice flights with them when he should have been attending to his job as an intelligence officer.

In 1949, the then Head of Historical Branch at the Air Ministry, John Nerney, was approached with a suggestion by John Pudney, who was involved in BBC Television at the time, that a book about 617 should be written by an Australian writer, Paul Brickhill. He had written a book with Conrad Norton called 'Escape to Danger' which was then being made into a TV series. Out of this came a book written by Brickhill in 1950 called 'The Dam Busters' published in 1951. From the book came a film also called 'The Dam Busters'. The filming began in 1953 and Wg Cdr Wally Dunn, the man who had taken the signal 'Nigger' some ten years before, was appointed as technical adviser. The film is a classic today and took a lot of constructing, particularly the attack on the dam itself, all set up in huge sheds with massive steel doors. The film cost £250,000 to make but it soon became a dollar-buster. The Warner brothers, who had first jeered at the film, were now cheering and booking it into a major circuit in America. It was to go on and break all records at the Empire, Leicester Square, and in Birmingham.

A reception was given on 14th May, prior the Premier, for the then current members of 617 Squadron, the RAF Association, British Pictures and the Pathfinder Association, held at the Louis

XV room at the Criterion Restaurant in London. A model, nine feet by three feet three inches, of the Möhne Dam was made by The Savings Branch of the RAF Association and was to be displayed at the Premier and wherever in the country the film was being shown. The part of Guy Gibson was played by Richard Todd, who had been in the Parachute Regiment during the war. He said he was very privileged to play Guy Gibson and to be associated with the squadron. He went on to say that he felt it was a classic of its time. It took two years to research and make to ensure it was factually correct. Todd spent a lot of time talking to various people who had known Gibson, his widow Eve, his father Alexander, Barnes Wallis, Mickey Martin, and many others - even his headmaster and scoutmaster. They soon realised they were dealing with a marvellous subject and it had to be done credibly and faithfully.

The film premier had to be done over two days, 16th and 17th May 1955, at the Empire Theatre, Leicester Square. On the 16th, 14 original members of 617 were introduced to Princess Margaret and also present on the 16th, were Eve[1] and Guy's father, Alexander. He said at the Premier 'He was a nice looking boy", and when he saw the signature on a photograph of Gibson, he recalled how Guy had said, after the raid, how sorry he was for the animals when the dams burst.

On the 17th, a further 12 original members of the squadron were introduced to the Duke and Duchess of Gloucester, including Tony Burcher and Freddie Tees, who had been shot down but survived to become prisoners, although both were badly injured, Tees having badly burnt. The film was based on Brickhill's book and Gibson's own book 'Enemy Coast Ahead' published in 1946.

A number of next of kin were present, including John

---

[1] - *By then Mrs Eve Hyman, having married a South African, Jack Hyman who was later killed in a car accident.*

Pulford's[2] brother. 1956 was the 100th Anniversary of the Victoria Cross being instituted and to mark the occasion an exhibition was held at Marlborough House. Guy Gibson's VC and other medals were on display, along with the Medallion of Freedom of Vancouver presented to him on his USA/Canada tour in 1943. The medals were loaned by his father, Alexander. A portrait of Gibson painted in oils was loaned by RAF Scampton and a model aircraft was loaned by his former wife.

On the 19th of May 1968, to mark the 25th Anniversary of the Dams raid, a service was held at St Clement Dane's, the Royal Air Force Church in the Strand. It had been preceded on the 18th by a reception and showing of the film at the Warner Theatre, Leicester Square, by Warner Pathe and British Picture Corporation. Afterwards a cocktail party was attended by many of the survivors, Barnes Wallis, Richard Todd, Sir Arthur Harris, Ralph Cochrane, and the former Station Commander, Charles Whitworth. One of the lessons at the service was read by Mick Martin.

In 1968, Guy's father, Alexander, died in Chelsea at the age of 94. In 1972, a reunion was organised in Canada and eleven of the 40 ex-members of the squadron present had been on the Dams raid. In 1976, the reunion was in Holland and on the 19th May a visit was paid to the graves of Guy Gibson and Jim Warwick, where wreaths were laid by Eve Gibson, and Miss Ellen Warwick, James Warwick's sister, plus many other individuals and organisations.

In 1977, a wonderful 90th Birthday party for Sir Barnes Wallis was attended by many former members of the squadron. Mrs Eve Gibson attended, having reverted back to being Gibson from Hyman by deed poll, Also present were Sir Arthur Harris, Sir Ralph Cochrane, and a number of ex members of 617 Squadron.

[2] - *Gibson's flight engineer on the raid.*

44 - Gibson's and Warwick's headstones as they are today. The grave has been carefully tended for the last twenty-five years by Mr van den Driesschen of Rotterdam. Standing behind Gibson's headstone is Len Sumpter, one of the few survivours of the Dams Raid who is still alive at the time of writing.

In 1979, a plaque was presented to the RAF Museum at Hendon in memory of Guy Gibson. It came from wartime Dutch Resistance Fighters and is now on permanent display at the museum.

In April 1980 the reunion was in Australia and while there the 617 Squadron contingent led the Anzac Parade in Adelaide.

In May 1980 a reunion was held in Derby, organised by the Derbyshire County Council and Rolls Royce Limited. During the two day visit a helicopter flight over the Derwent Dam, which had been used for the Dams training back in 1943, was arranged and a poppy wreath dropped in memory of the men lost on the Dams raid.

During 1980 a bust of Guy Gibson was presented by a Dutch couple to 617 Squadron Association.

In January 1981, a gold cigarette case which had been presented to Guy Gibson in 1943 and was inscribed *ED932-G[3] G.P.G, May 17th, 1943. "Nigger" "Dinghy"* was sold in auction at Sotherby's. It had been estimated to sell for £600, but in fact went for £4,600, which shows the interest even 38 years after the raid on the Dams and the death of Guy Gibson.

A road on the South Candford Heath Estate has been named after Guy Gibson along with many other famous airmen. In 1979, George Brookes the President of the Birmingham Dahlia Society, named a dahlia after Guy Gibson - it was salmon pink. He also brought one out for Barnes Wallis in yellow, both measuring eight to twelve inches. George had spent his war in bomb disposal all over the UK.

In 1983, came the 40th Anniversary of the Dams raid and a week of celebrations in Lincoln. It was a great pleasure to see Les Munro all the way from New Zealand.

In May 1987, at Woodhall Spa, a memorial was unveiled in the form of the Möhne Dam on which are the names of 201 men

---

[3] - *The number of Gibson's Lancaster on the Dams raid.*

of 617 Sqdn who were killed in the war, one of course being Guy Gibson. After the unveiling the choir from a local school, St Hugh's, were seated in front of the memorial and the school PE teacher, Mark Upton, decided to take a photograph of the choir. As he did a black labrador dog sat in the middle of the choir and refused to go away. Guy's dog, Nigger, was a black labrador. After the photograph had been taken the dog went off and has never been seen again. It was as if Nigger had come back to say he was a part of 617 Squadron and should be there on the day. Maybe, in hindsight, his name should have been on the Roll of Honour too. One thing is certain: whenever the story of the Dambusters and Guy Gibson is told the name 'Nigger' will always be a part of it.

In Holland, the graves of Guy Gibson and Jim Warwick have been a place for thousands of people to visit over many years. In September 1989, the 45th Anniversary of his death, controversy surrounded a memorial which was unveiled in the Porthleven Cemetery, in Cornwall. The memorial was originally to be sited adjacent to the town's war memorial, but permission was withdrawn by the local council at the last moment. The whole conception of the memorial had been the brainchild of the Chairman of the Council, Michael Gale, and as a result of the council's action he resigned. He had formerly served as a tank driver and seen service in the Middle East and Northwest Europe. At the last minute the memorial was erected in the cemetery and the unveiling was done by Gibson's cousin, Janet de Gaynesford. Janet still has a set of wings Guy wore and also a brooch he gave her before the Dams raid in 1943.

Alick, Guy's brother died in 1988, his son is named Michael Penrose Gibson, Penrose, of course, being Guy's second christian name. In October 1988, Guy's wife Eve died after a long illness and fight against cancer. She had retired in 1980 from her job as deputy head housekeeper at Claridge's Hotel and in her will she bequeathed Guy's medals to the RAF Museum, Hendon, where they now reside. Alongside his medals are the medals of his comrade in arms on the Dams raid, Mick Martin, who died in 1989.

On 5th May 1989, a memorial was unveiled in the Steenbergen park by Leonard Cheshire, the conception and planning of which was solely one man's - Albert Postma. The memorial is a seven foot obelisk on which has been mounted a three-bladed propeller. The propeller is from a former 106 Squadron Lancaster R5697 that had crashed in Holland on 21st December 1942, while being flown by a Sgt George Anderson. On the memorial is an inscription:

FOR OUR TOMORROW THEY GAVE THEIR TODAY LEST WE FORGET

There are also the crests of 106 and 617 Squadrons, Gibson's old squadrons. Albert himself was a member of the Dutch Resistance Group and fought with the 82nd Airborne Division at Nijmegen.

Gibson had surprising sides to his character. In his room was a complete set of Shakespeare, and at the end of a conference with one of his squadron commanders he would suddenly take down one of his volumes of Shakespeare and say 'This is a wonderful bit', and begin reading out a favourite passage, he would compare people with Shakespearean characters.

The scouts in Maidstone where Gibson had reaffirmed his scouts oath said of him:

> 'From every point of view he was a remarkable
> man and would have gone far in any walk of
> life. He will long be remembered in the group in
> which he served for his infectious enthusiasm,
> his determination to surmount any and every
> difficulty, and his sound common sense.'

They have a cave which serves as a chapel and on the side of the altar stand six memorial crosses for six Rover Scouts of the 1st Tovil Troop who fell in the war. The cross in the middle is higher, but only a shade, than the others. On it is inscribed simply 'Guy Gibson.'

Sir Ralph Cochrane described him as, 'a chunky little man who would be the obvious choice for senior prefect at any school, a natural leader who did not look for easy solutions.'

'Chiefy' Powell said: 'There was a tremendous spirit among the men under Wing Commander Guy Gibson - he was the finest commander I had ever served under. Guy Gibson gave me the fuse key, and I have treasured it ever since. It is my most prized possession.'

Lastly, Sir Arthur Harris said of him, 'His natural aptitude for leadership, his outstanding skill, and his extraordinary valour marked him early for command; his personal contribution towards victory was beyond doubt unsurpassed.'

Perhaps Gibson's most lasting and fitting epitaph is that even after the passage of fifty years his name is still a household word and, for the men who served with him, there is the enduring memory of a born leader and an outstanding flyer.

Today, there are only 23 survivors of the Dams raid alive and of them only 4 of the 19 pilots who set out on that night 50 years ago.

Appendix I - *Curriculum Vitae*

39438 Wing Commander Guy Penrose Gibson

Granted a short service commission for 4 years.	31.1.37.
With effect as a Pilot Officer	16.11.36.
Posted to Civil Flying School (Yatesbury) Depot No 24 Training Group.	31.1.37.
No 6 Flying Training School (Netheravon)	6.2.37.
No 5 Course Under Flying Instruction.	
Presented with Wings	27.5.37.
83 Bomber Squadron No 2 Group (Scampton)	4.9.37.
No 3 School of Technical Training - Parachute Training	27.9.37.
No 24 Training Group - Navigation Course Hamble	19.2.39.
Blind Approach Course	27.3.40 to 5.4.40.
No 14. Operational Training Unit (Cottesmore)	26.9.40.
No 16. Operational Training Unit (Upper Heyford)	11.10.40.
29 Fighter Squadron (West Malling)	13.11.40.
No 51 Operatinal Training Unit (Cranfield) - Instructor	23.12.41.
No 51 HQ Group	23.3.42.
106 Bomber Squadron (Syerston) - Commanding Officer	13.4.42.
No 5 Group Bomber Command	15.3.43.

APPENDIX I

617 Bomber Squadron (Scampton)	24.3.43.
Ministry of Information Lecture Tour	3.8.43.
Left for USA/Canada	5.8.43.
Air Ministry Directive Prevention Accidents -	3.1.44.
Deputy director	
RAF Uxbridge 28 Group Course	13.3.44.
No 12. War Staff Course	
No 54 Base 5 Group (Coningsby) -	12.6.44.
Staff Officer	
Missing / Killed Flying a Mosquito of 627 Sqdn.	
from Woodhall Spa.	19.9.44.

Promoted F/O	16.6.39.
" F/Lt	3.9.40.
Transferred to the RAFVR retained on the active	
list his four years being up.	16.11.40.
A/Sqdn Ldr	1.12.41.
Sqdn Ldr (War Substantive)	13.4.42.
Acting Wing Commander	13.4.42.

156612. A/Squadron Leader James Brown Warwick

Born Belfast 10 of October 1921.

No 1 Aircrew Reception Centre	1.9.1941.
No 3 Initial Training Wing	20.9.1941.
No 1 Empire Air Observers School	17.1.1942.
No 31 Royal Air Force Personnel Depot	26.3.1942.
Moncton, Canada.	
Miami, USA	19.4. to 12.5.1942
No 3 Personnel Reception Centre (UK)	7.10.1942.
RCAF Reception Centre	8.10.1942.
No 3 Observers Advanced Flying Unit	3.12.1942.
No 19 Operational Training Unit	26.1.1943.
No 1661 Conversion Unit	18.4.1943.
No 49 Squadron	29.5.1943.
No 1485 Bombing and Gunnery Flight Badney	14.1.1944.
No 1661. Conversion Unit	5.2.1944.
No 54 Base Coningsby	25.8.1944.
Missing	19.9.1944.
Leading Aircraftman	29.11.1941.
Temp Sergeant / Navigator	25.1.1943.
Pilot Officer	4.8.1943.
Flying Officer	4.2.1944.
Acting/Flight Lieutenant	5.2.1944.
Acting / Squadron Leader	25.8.1944.

APPENDIX II

The crews for 'Operation Chastise'

A' FLIGHT

Pilot:	W/C G P Gibson	S/L H M Young
F/Eng:	Sgt J Pulford	Sgt D T Horsfall
Nav:	P/O H T Taerum	Sgt C W Roberts
W/Opt:	F/L R E G Hutchison	Sgt L W Nichols
B/A :	P/O F M Spafford	F/O V S MacCausland
F/Gnr:	F/Sgt G A Deering	Sgt G A Yeo
R/Gnr:	F/L R A D Trevor-Roper	Sgt W Ibbotson

F/Lt W Astell	F/Lt D J Maltby
Sgt J Kinnear	Sgt W Hatton
P/O F A Wile	Sgt V Nicholson
Sgt A Garshowitz	Sgt A J Stone
F/O D Hopkinson	P/O J Fort
Sgt F A Garbas	F/Sgt V Hill
Sgt R Bolitho	Sgt H T Simmonds

F/Lt D J Shannon	F/Lt R N G Barlow
Sgt R J Henderson	Sgt S L Whillis
P/O D R Walker	F/O P S Burgess
F/O B Goodale	F/O C R Williams
F/Sgt L J Sumpter	Sgt A Gillespie
Sgt B Jagger	F/O H S Glinz
P/O J Buckley	Sgt J R G Liddell

P/O G Rice
Sgt E C Smith
F/O R MacFarlane
Sgt C B Gowrie
F/Sgt J W Thrasher
Sgt T W Maynard
Sgt S Burns

P/O W Ottley
Sgt R Marsden
F/O J K Barrett
Sgt J Guterman
F/Sgt T B Johnston
Sgt H J Strange
F/Sgt F Tees

F/Sgt K W Brown
Sgt H B Feneron
Sgt D P Heal
Sgt H J Hewstone
Sgt S Oancia
Sgt D Allatson
F/Sgt G S McDonald

Sgt V W Byers
Sgt A J Taylor
P/O J H Warner
Sgt J Wilkinson
Sgt A N Whittaker
Sgt c Mc A Jarvie
Sgt J McDowell

Crew not used:

P/O W G Divall
Sgt D W Warwick
Sgt J S Simpson
Sgt R C McArthur
Sgt   Murray
Sgt E C A Balke
Sgt A A Williams

'B' FLIGHT

S/L H E Maudsley
Sgt J Marriott
F/O R A Urquhart
Sgt A P Cottam
P/O M J D Fuller
F/O W J Tytherleigh
Sgt N R Burrows

F/Lt J V Hopgood
Sgt C Brennan
F/O K Earnshaw
Sgt J W Minchin
P/O J W Fraser
P/O G H F G Gregory
F/O A F Burcher

F/Lt H B Martin
P/O I Whittaker
F/Lt J F Leggo
F/O L Chambers
F/Lt R C Hay
P/O B T Foxlee
F/Sgt T D Simpson

F/Lt J C McCarthy
Sgt W Radcliffe
F/Sgt D A McLean
Sgt L Eaton
Sgt G L Johnson
Sgt R Batson
F/O D Rodger

F/Lt L G Knight
Sgt R E Grayston
F/O H S Hobday
Sgt R G T Kellow
F/O E C Johnson
Sgt F E Sutherland
Sgt H E O'Brien

F/Sgt C T Anderson
Sgt R C Paterson
Sgt J P Nugent
Sgt W D Bickle
Sgt G J Green
Sgt E Ewan
Sgt A W Buck

F/Lt J L Munro
Sgt F E Appleby
F/O F G Rumbles
Sgt P E Pigeon
Sgt J H Clay
Sgt W Howarth
F/Sgt H A Weeks

P/O L J Burpee
Sgt G Pegler
Sgt T Jaye
P/O L G Weller
Sgt J L Arthur
Sgt W C A Long
F/Sgt J G Brady

F/Sgt W C Townsend
Sgt D J D Powell
P/O C L Howard
F/Sgt G A Chalmers
Sgt C E Franklin
Sgt D E Webb
Sgt R Wilkinson

Crew not used:
F/Lt H S Wilson
Sgt T W Johnson
F/O J A Rodger
Sgt L Mieyette
P/O S H Coles
Sgt T H Payne
Sgt E Hornby

'A' Flight Bombing Leader   -   F/O Johnston,
    Flight Gunnery Leader   -   F/O Glinz
    Flight Navigation Leader -   F/O MacFarlane
'B' Flight Bombing Leader   -   F/O Johnson
    Flight Gunnery Leader   -   F/O Tytherleigh
    Flight Navigation Leader -   F/O Urquhart

Sqdn Signals Leader -   F/Lt Hutchison
Bombing Leader   -   F/Lt Hay
Gunnery Leader   -   F/Lt Trevor-Roper
Navigation Leader   -   F/Lt Leggo
Flight Eng Leader   -   Sgt Johnson

Appendix III

Aircraft flown operationally by Wg Cdr Guy Gibson

Hampdens - 83 Sqdn

L. 4070 --- Contracted to 83 Sqdn 9.1.1939. Lost 7.5.41.
Aircraft crashed and burnt out with 14 OTU.

L. 4055 --- Contracted to 83 Sqdn 25.11.38
left 83 Sqdn 6.6.40.

L. 4049 --- Contracted to 83 31.10.38.
missing 24.9.40 Berlin.

X. 2897 --- Contracted to 83 Sqdn 21.8.40.

P. 4402 --- Contracted to 83 Sqdn 16.7.40.
Crashed and burnt out 9.11.40.

P. 1183 --- Contracted to 83 Sqdn 30.8.40.

Beaufighters - 29 Squadron.

R. 2150 --- Contracted to 29 Sqdn 16.11.40.
Crashed and burnt out 15.2.41.

R. 2196 --- Contracted to 29 Sqdn 4.1.41.
Crashed 11.2.41.

R. 2144 --- Contracted to 29 Sqdn 15.11.40.
Crashed and burnt out 23.12.41.

R. 2128 --- Contracted to 29 Sqdn 2.1.41.

R. 2094 --- Contracted to 29 Sqdn 24.10.40.
Scrapped 2.7.45.

R. 2205 --- Contracted to 29 Sqdn 28.2.41.
Scrapped 29.11.45.

R. 2280 --- Down as a 600 Sqdn aircraft 16.6.41.

Manchesters 106 Squadron

R. 5770 ---   Contracted to 106 Sqdn 15.4.42.
                         Scrapped 13.7.43.

L. 7378 ---   Previously with 207 Sqdn 13.4.41 to 106
                         12.3.42.

Lancasters 106 Squadron

R. 5681 ---   Contracted to 106 Sqdn 19.6.42.
                         Missing 17.9.42 a Raid on Essen.

R. 5670 ---   Contracted to 106 Sqdn 11.6.42
                         Crashed and burnt 7.11.42.

R. 5899 ---   Contracted to 106 Sqdn 29.7.42.
                         Missing 18.9.42 Mining Operation to
                         Danzig. Crash landed in the sea.

R. 5901 ---   Contracted to 106 Sqdn 4.8.42
                         To 44 Sqdn 5.4.43. Scrapped 26.10.43.

R. 5551 ---   Previously with 97 Sqdn 1.5.42
                         to 106 Sqdn 29.5.42. Missing 15.6.43.

R. 5492 ---   Previously with 44 Sqdn to 106 Sqdn
                         22.10.42. Crashed and burnt 4.9.43.

L. 7579 ---   Contracted to 106 Sqdn 10.5.42

W. 4118 - Y   Contracted to 106 Sqdn 6.8.42
                         Missing 4.2.43 operation to Turin
                         but crashed in France. Known as Admiral
                         Prune.

W. 4102   Contracted to 106 Sqdn 28.7.42
                                Crashed and burnt 5.10.42.

R. 5611   Contracted to 106 Sqdn 24.10.42
                                Missing 17.5.43.

Lancaster 617 Squadron

ED 932-G   Contracted to 617 Sqdn 30.4.43
                                Used on Dams Raid 16/17 May 43.
                                To 467 Sqdn 7.2.45
                                To 61 Sqdn 27.8.46
                                Scrapped 29.7.47.

Appendix IV

Wartime Operations - Wing Commander GP Gibson

83 Squadron

(1) 3:9:39
Attack the German Fleet entrance to the Kiel Canal. Aborted due to bad weather.
Crew: P/O Warner, Sgt Houghton, AC Hewit

(2) 27:2:40
North Sea sweep looking for U-Boats
Crew: AC McCormack replaced Hewitt, P/O Withers replaced Warner.

(3) 29:2:40
North Sea sweep.
Crew: Same

(4) 11/12:4:40
Recce. Fredrick Middlefart, Little Belt, Kattergart, Kiel Harbour.
Crew: Same

(5) 14/15:4:40
Gardening Middlefart Bridge successfully placed carrot.
Crew: P/O Watson replaced Houghton.

(6) 20/21:4:40
Aalborg Airfield
Crew: Same

(7) 23/24:4:40
Gardening (Mine Laying)
Crew: Same

(8) 14/15:5:40
Copenhagen lettuce dropping

(9) 17/18:5:40
Hamburg attacked successfully hit a balloon cable starboard wing
Crew: Same

(10) 22/23:5:40
Railway Bridge over Schelde-Maas which was destroyed
Crew: Same

(11) 26/27:5:40
Entrance to the railway line near Aachen
Crew: Same

(12) 30/31:5:40
Oil tanks NE of Brunsbuttel unable to identify bombs brought back.
Crew: Same

(13) 9/10:6:40
Gardening
Crew: Same

(14) 11/12:6:40
Target not located bombed
Flushing airfield instead
Crew: Same

(15) 13/14:6:40
Target Hirson not located
bombed road junction 30
miles east of target.
Crew: Same

(16) 17/18:6:40
Oil refinery Hannover
Crew: Same

(17) 19/20:6:40
Road junction successfully
bombed
Crew: Same

(18) 21/22:6:40
Aircraft factory Kassel
Crew: Same

(19) 23/24:6:40
Factory Wismar
Crew: Same

(20) 27/28:6:40
Same factory as previous
Op.
Crew: Same

(21) 29/30:6:40
Gardening
Crew: Same

(22) 1/2:7:40
Kiel Docks
Crew: Same

(23) 4/5:7:40
Kiel
Crew: Same

(24) 9/10:7:40
Wilhelmshaven
Crew: Same

(25) 15/16:7:40
Simor NE of Dortmund
Crew: Same

(26) 26/27:7:40
Oil refinery Nantes
Crew: Same

(27) 28/29:7:40
Frankfurt
Crew: Same

(28) 24/25:8:40
Target D4 not indicated
bombs brought back
Crew: Same

(29) 27/28:8:40
Gardening Lorient bombs
brought back an E-Boat
attacked
Crew: Same

(30) 1:9:40
Marshalling yards -
Germany
Crew: Same

(31) 5:9:40
A high dive made on a ship
near Elbe Bruns Butter
Crew: Same

(32) 7:9:40
Barges Ostend
Crew: Same

---

(33) 15:9:40
Barges Antwerp attacked
from 800 feet one bomb
dropped on a barge up river.
Same operation as Sgt
Hannah awarded VC.
Crew: Same

---

(34) 18:9:40
Viaduct Dormund-Emms
canal
Crew: Same

---

(35) 20:9:40
Dortmund-Emms Canal a
shell went through the
cockpit and knocked out the
intercom system
Crew: Same

---

(36) 23:9:40
Potsdam Station Berlin
Crew: Same

Last operation with 83
Squadron - Total Flown 36.

Posted 14 OTU Cottesmore

(1) 19:11:40
X Raid Patrol (Blenheim)
Crew: P/O Watson

---

29 Squadron (Beaufighters)

(2) 10:12:40
Patrol
Crew: Sgt Taylor Ai
operator

---

(3) 11:12:40
X Raid - Ju 88 Attacked
Crew: Same

---

(4) 12:12:40
X Raid
Crew: P/O Watson

---

(5) 12:12:40
X Raid
Crew: Same

---

(6) 20:12:40
X Raid - He111 seen
Crew: P/O Francombe

---

(7) 20:12:40
X Raid
Crew: Same

---

(8) 23:12:40
X Raid - R/T Packed up
Crew: A/C Taylor

---

(9) 22:1:41
X Raid
Crew: Sgt Parr

---

(10) 31:1:41
X Raid
Crew: Sgt Ashworth

---

(11) 31:1:41
X Raid
Crew: Same

---

(12) 1:2:41
Day Op. Contact which was
a Blenheim
Crew: Sgt James

---

(13) 4:2:41
X Raid - E.Aircraft attacked
Crew: Sgt James

---

(14) 5:2:41
X Raid - 3 blips!
Crew: Same

---

(15) 9:2:41
X Raid - Ai U/S
Crew: Same

---

(16) 10:2:41
Dawn Patrol - Flushing/Den
Helder
Crew: Same

---

(17) 14:2:41
X Raid
Crew: Sgt Austin

---

(18) 2:3:41
Dusk patrol
Crew: Sgt James

---

(19) 6:3:41
X Raid
Crew: P/O Watson

---

(20) 7:3:41
X Raid
Crew: Same

---

(21) 12:3:41
X Raid - One Hun destroyed
Crew: Sgt James

---

(22) 13:3:41
X Raid
Crew: Same

---

(23) 14:3:41
X Raid - Heinkel 111
Crew: Same

---

(24) 4:4:41
X Raid - Nothing about
Crew: Sgt Ryall

---

(25) 8:4:41
X Raid - Shot up when
landing
Crew: Sgt Bell wounded
Crashed on landing

---

(26) 10:4:41
X Raid - Wireless U/S
Crew: Sgt Taylor

---

(27) 16:4:41
X Raid - Saw nought
Crew: Sgt James

---

(28) 16:4:41
X Raid - G.C.I. practice
too.
Crew: Sgt James

---

(29) 23:4:41
X Raid - A great night. 10 blips 2 visuals.
Hit second and damaged it.
Return fire quite
frightening -
Crew: Same

---

(30) 3:5:41
X Raid - Nothing
Crew: Same

---

(31) 7:5:41
X Raid - One destroyed by lucky burst. It blew
up. Another did the same before I could open fire!
Crew: Same

---

(32) 9:5:41
X Raid - Stooging
Crew: Same

---

(33) 10:5:41
X Raid - A Blitz on London. Saw two HE 111 -
 but cannons
would not fire. Damaged one with Brownings - No claim.
Crew: Same

---

(34) 23:5:41
X Raid - Returned
Crew: P/O Willis

---

(35) 1:6:41
X Raid
Crew: Sgt James

---

(36) 11:6:41
X Raid - 3 Blips
Crew: P/O Willis

---

(37) 13:6:41
X Raid
Crew: Same

---

(38) 17:6:41
X Raid
Crew: Sgt James

---

(39) 23:6:41
X Raid - Ai U/S
Crew: Same

---

(40) 25:6:41
X Raid - Nothing
Crew: Same

---

(41) 2:7:41
X Raid
Crew: Same

---

(42) 4:7:41
X Raid
Crew: Same

---

(43) 5:7:41
X Raid
Crew: Same

---

(44) 6:7:41
X Raid - One Heinkel 111 destroyed off Sheerness -
Blew up
Crew: Same

(45) 10:7:41
X Raid
Crew: Same

(46) 12:7:41
X Raid - G.C.I 3 visual.
Crew: Same

(47) 17:7:41
X Raid
Crew: Same

(48) 22:7:41
Patrol
Crew: Same

(49) 27:7:41
X Raid - R/T. F.
Crew: Same

(50) 27:7:41
X Raid
Crew: Same

(51) 29:7:41
X Raid Patrol
Crew: Same

(52) 10:8:41
Ai Patrol - Le Touquet
Crew: Same

(53) 22:8:41
G.C.I
Crew: same

(54) 25:8:41
Ai
Crew: Same

(55) 25:8:41
Patrol
Crew: Same

(56) 26:8:41
Patrol and searchlight co.op
Crew: Same

(57) 28:8:41
G.C.I
Crew: Same

(58) 28:8:41
Patrol
Crew: Same

(59) 29:8:41
Patrol
Crew: Same

(60) 29:8:41
Patrol
Crew: Same

(61) 1:9:41
X Raid
Crew: Same

(62) 2:9:41
Stooge Patrol
Crew: Same

(63) 11:9:41
Stooge Patrol
Crew: Same

(64) 12:9:41
'Operation Gibson' and X Raid
Crew: Same

(65) 13:9:41
'Operation Gibson' and X Raid
Crew: Same

(66) 15:9:41
X Raid - Two Blips
Crew: Same

(67) 16:9:41
X Raid Patrol. One Blip.
Crew: Same

(68) 18:9:41
Ai Patrol
Crew: Same

(69) 29:9:41
Ai
Crew: Same

(70) 29:9:41
Patrol - Saw Heinchel
Crew: Same

(71) 1:10:41
Patrol
Crew: Same

(72) 3:10:41
Patrol - No Huns.
Crew: Same

(73) 21:10:41
B/A + Ai
Crew: Same

(74) 21:10:41
G.C.I. + Ai
Crew: Same

(75) 21:10:41
X Raid - Saw and damaged two Ju87's off Dover.
Crew: Same

(76) 24:10:41
G.C.I
Crew: Same

(77) 25:10:41
B/A + Ai
Crew: same

(78) 25:10:41
Patrol. Nothing
Crew: Same

(79) 26:10:41
Ai
Crew: Same

(80) 26:10:41
Patrol - Nothing
Crew: Same

(81) 31:10:41
Patrol - Nothing
Crew: Same

(82) 2:11:41
Patrol - G.C.I
Crew: same

(83) 3:11:41
G.C.I + Ai
Crew: Same

(84) 6:11:41
X Raid
Crew: Same

(85) 10:11:41
Patrol - Estuary
Crew: Same

(86) 12:11:41
Patrol - Two intercepts
Crew: Same

(87) 17:11:41
X Raid - Two Blips. Filthy
W. (weather)
Crew: Sgt Miller

(88) 20:11:41
Patrol
Crew: F/O Willis

(89) 21:11:41
Ai
Crew: Same

(90) 21:11:41
Patrol - Two visuals Beau.
Crew: Same

(91) 27:11:41
Patrol. Queer Control.
Crew: Same

(92) 5:12:41
Ai - G.C
Crew: Same

(93) 8:12:41
Patrol. Nothing about.
Crew: Sgt James

(94) 9:12:41
G.C.I. + Ai
Crew: Same

(95) 10:12:41
Ai + BA
Crew: Same

(96) 11:12:41
G.C.I
Crew: Same

(97) 11:12:41
X Raid Patrol
Crew: Same

(98) 15:12:41
X Raid Patrol - Nothing
about
Crew: Same

(99) 15:12:41
X Raid - Nothing about
Crew: Same

Total sorties 99

106 Squadron

22/23:4:42
Gardening Radishes

25/26:4:42
Rostock attacked from 3,500
feet.
Good results

4/5:5:42
Minelaying off Sylt.

8/9:5:42
Heinkel works Wernemunde
from 3,500 feet

Converted to Lancasters

8:7:42
Wilmenshaven 10,000 ft.
Load 5 X 2,000 HE
'Good Prang'

11:7:42
Daylight raid on.
Load 5 X 1000
Missed a ship in harbour by
20 yds from 1,000 feet.

18:7:42
Essen. Recalled bombs
jettisoned.

26/27:7:42
700 aircraft on Hamburg.
Large fires burning all over
town. Flak very intense and
we nearly bought it coming
out at Brunsbuttel.

31:7:42
Dusseldorf collected a
packet from 500 aircraft.
Load 1 X 4000 + 12 SBC.
Height 12,000.

8/9:8:42
Operations mining Skaw.

10:8:42
Operations mining Baltic.

12:8:42
Mainz. We bombed from
5,000' under cloud. Load 5
X 2000lb.

27:8:42
A special raid on Gydnia
where three German
warships were lying.
Attacked from all heights 6 -
12,000 ft.

1:9:42
Saabruchen

13:9:42
Bombing Bremen. A very
hot target. Lost 10%
attacking force.

23:9:42
Dornier factory Wismar

15:10:42
Cologne. Hit by flak

17:10:42
Daylight low level attack on the transformer station at Le Cruesot. Bombed at 500 feet and recieved a few bullet holes.

22/23:10:42
Genoa

24:10:42
Milan. Daylight raid. Bombed from 5,000 feet

Crew: Sgt Pegler, P/O Rushell, F/Sgt Lewis, P/O Hutchinson, P/O Wickens, F/Ltn Oliver.

6:11:42
Genoa

18:11:42
Turin - Fiat works

28:11:42
Turin

11:1:43
Essen

17:1:43
Berlin - carried Richard Dimbleby who recorded the trip on a record. Crew changes: Sub Lt. Mutrie RN bomb aimer, Sgt McGregor rear gunner.

14:2:43
Milan

25:2:43
Nuremburg

Crew: F/Lt Burnside, F.Lt Oliver, F/O Wickens, Sgt Britton, F/Lt Lodge, P/O Hutchinson

---

26:2:43
Cologne - 'Wizard Prang' 169th Wartime flight.

11:3:43
Stuttgart
Crew: P/O Thompson, Sub Lt Muttrie, F/Lt Scrivenor, F/Lt Oliver, Sgt Hartgreaves, Sgt Hayhurst
Last operation with 106 Squadron and 71st on bombers.

Summary of Operational Flying:

1st Tour Hampdens - 242 hrs .20 mins   42 Sorties (4 Day)

2nd Tour Beaufighters 199 hrs .10 mins 99 Sorites (19 Day)

3rd Tour Manch/Lancasters 201 hrs 29 Sorties (4 Day)

Total: 642.30 hrs 170 Ops.

---

617 Squadron

16/17:5:43

Ruhr Dams

Crew: Sgt Pulford, P/O Deering, F.Lt Trevor-Roper, F.Lt Hutchinson, P/O Spafford, P/O Taerum.

Awarded Victoria Cross 23:5:43

2:8:43
Attack on special objectives with Wg Cdr Holden

19:7:44
An operation with 630 Sqdn target Creil NW Paris

18:8:44
An operation to Deelan Airfield in a Lightning

10:9:44
An operation to LeHavre in a Mosquito

19:9:44
An operation to Munchen Gladbach and Rheydt in a Mosquito from 627 Squadron.
Crew: S/L Warwick DFC

Missing.

'SPITFIRE ON MY TAIL'

A View From The Other Side

Ulrich Steinhilper & Peter Osborne

Non-fiction   *Illustrated*

ISBN 1 872836 003

Spitfire On My Tail is the detailed account of how one German grew up and joined the *Luftwaffe* as a career officer and airman. It was written by Ulrich Steinhilper who was an *Oberleutnant* with JG 52 (52nd Fighter Wing) based at Coquelles near Calais. He flew over one-hundred and fifty combat missions during the Battle of Britain and saw his *Gruppe* of thirty-six experienced pilots whittled down to just a handful by October.

It is a very personal and human story of the naivety of youth being shaped by the forces of war. Poignant lessons learned by tragic accidents, counterbalanced by anger towards those who saw the war as a means of personal advancement and self aggrandizement.

There is no doubt there is, today, a movement towards a more balanced understanding of events and *SPITFIRE ON MY TAIL*, already being referred to as a classic of the period, presents a rare opportunity for students of this classic air engagement to see The View From The Other Side. In a market where new books on the subject, and many re-issues of classics, offer a bewildering choice *SPITFIRE ON MY TAIL* is in a class of its own.

'SPITFIRE ON MY TAIL': 335 Pages, 84 black & white illustrations, hardback only. Price: £14.95 inc p & p

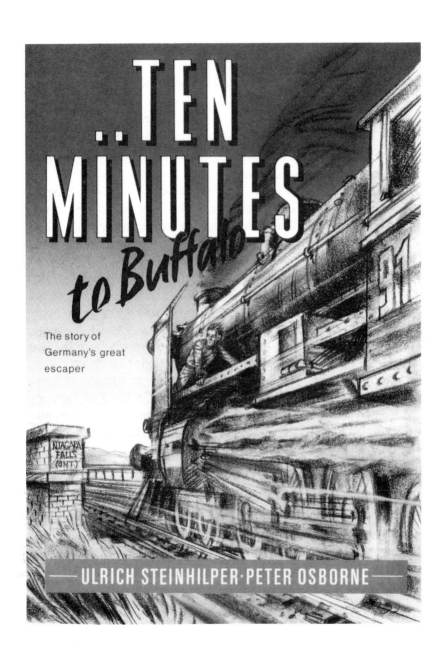

..TEN MINUTES
MINUTES
to Buffalo

The story of
Germany's great
escaper

NIAGARA
FALLS
(ONT)

91

— ULRICH STEINHILPER·PETER OSBORNE —

'TEN MINUTES TO BUFFALO'

The Story of Germany's Great Escaper

Ulrich Steinhilper & Peter Osborne

Non-Fiction   *Illustrated*

ISBN 1 872836 01 1

"Ten Minutes to Buffalo" is long-awaited sequel to Ulrich Steinhilper's highly successful first book, "Spitfire On My Tail". Unlike the first book, which tells the story of how a young German came to fly in Hitler's Luftwaffe and to fight in the Battle of Britain, "Ten Minutes to Buffalo" is a catalogue of courage and determination on the ground. In this way it is set to repeat the successful formula by providing a rare chance to witness how things were for 'The Other Side,' this time behind the barbed wire and in Ulrich Steinhilper's case - all too often outside the wire! It relates a story of remarkable courage and perseverance in the most appalling conditions, braving arctic weather and appalling hardship with one thought in mind - to get home.

From his first camp in England away to the vastness of Canada he and a select few of his fellow officers were to become known as *Die Ausbrecherkönige von Kanada* (the breakout kings from Canada) and Ulrich was to shine among them. His escapes were innovative and even audacious and it was only bad luck that seemed to keep him from a completely successful 'homerun'.

Very little has ever been written about the conditions of German officers as prisoners of the Allies and practically nothing of their ingenuity and perseverance in planning and executing escape plans so similar to their counterparts in German hands. This remarkable book is entirely written from original hand-written sheets which date from 1942 and which give it a great immediacy and accuracy.

'TEN MINUTES TO BUFFALO' 431 Pages, 45 black & white illustrations, hardback only. Price: £14.95 inc p & p